Distant

"This is a beautifully ingenious memoir, saturated in the history of the European 20th century, and made all the more compelling by Ann Goldstein's luminous translation."

VIVIAN GORNICK

"This stunning autobiography is both a love letter to a flawed and vanished childhood and a map of a woman's inner topography as she fumbles toward identity. Never before translated into English, Jarre is a wonderful new discovery."

WORDS WITHOUT BORDERS

"This impressionistic memoir by an overlooked Italian writer—the child of a Christian mother and a Jewish father killed in the Holocaust—is seen as her masterwork."

NEW YORK TIMES

"*Distant Fathers* is the first of [Jarre's] books available in English. It must not be the last … Written in lucid, luminous prose … she conceives of her life in terms of a darkness broken by occasional bursts of illumination."

LOS ANGELES REVIEW OF BOOKS

"Marina Jarre is an original, powerful and incisive writer … Her works—true, small-scale, essential masterpieces—have found passionate readers and critics and have an indisputable place in Italian literature of the past fifty years."

CLAUDIO MAGRIS

"Marina Jarre's astonishing work reads like a dreamscape. Here, a Nabokovian memory mingles with meditations on homeland, womanhood, and sexuality. A book both sharp as a blade and glistening like a river in the sun."

Lila Azam Zanganeh

"Like Nabokov's *Speak, Memory*, this book is more concerned with time and perspective than narrative storytelling, though Jarre is more like Ferrante in her lack of nostalgia and unflinching focus on the difficulties of relationships."

Kirkus

"Marina Jarre's vibrant memoir is stunning in its intimacy, honesty, and finely observed detail."

Hilma Wolitzer

"It's an incalculable source of joy when ... one of the greatest writers of the twentieth century can resume dialogue with the readers of today."

Il Libraio

Marina Jarre
Distant Fathers
A Memoir

Translated by
Ann Goldstein

HEAD
ZEUS

An Apollo Book

First published in Italian as *I padri lontani*

First published in English in the US in 2021 by New Vessel Press

First published in the UK in 2022 by Head of Zeus Ltd
This paperback edition first published in 2023 by Head of Zeus Ltd,
part of Bloomsbury Publishing Plc

9 7 5 3 1 2 4 6 8

A catalogue record for this book is available from the British Library.

ISBN (PB): 9781803280950
ISBN (E): 9781803280929

Front Cover: Milan (Italy), Sforza Castle, 1956. (Photo by
Mario De Biasi per Mondadori Portfolio via Getty Images)
Back Cover: Milan, 1950s (Photo by Mario De Biasi
per Mondadori Portfolio via Getty Images)

Printed and bound by CPI Group (UK) Ltd, Croydon, CR0 4YY

MIX
Paper | Supporting
responsible forestry
FSC® C171272
www.fsc.org

Head of Zeus Ltd
First Floor East
5–8 Hardwick Street
London EC1R 4RG

www.headofzeus.com

Table of Contents

Translator's Note

M arina Jarre's *Distant Fathers* tells the story of the author's life, but there is very little about the telling that is straightforward. The reader is thrown immediately into a city, Turin, that is not Jarre's place of birth or origin, as a way into the sensation of disorientation and displacement—the feeling of not belonging—that perpetually haunted her. It's as if she wanted readers, too, to have a direct experience of dislocation, of not knowing where they are. Gradually, she begins to find her way around the city, and we follow—but then suddenly she throws us off again by talking about the fantasies of a child running away from home: "Italy was the country I would have liked to escape to." And then, after the long swirling sentences of a woman wandering around Turin, we are startled by a short factual statement: "My sister and I were born in Riga."

This is Jarre's method, to keep confounding us with sudden changes of pace and tone and abrupt shifts in subject that digress but always circle back, creating a kind of tightly controlled stream of consciousness.

Some facts: Jarre's mother was Italian, from Torre Pellice, a town in the mountain valleys of Piedmont, southwest of Turin, and her father a Latvian-Russian Jew who was killed, along with the rest of his family, by the Nazis in 1941. Jarre (1925–2016) spent her first ten years in Riga, until her parents divorced and she was taken to live with her maternal grandmother in Torre Pellice. The first part of *Distant Fathers* recounts her childhood in Riga; the second part begins when she arrives at her grandmother's house, at the age of ten, and continues until she is twenty and a university student. The third part describes her marriage, children, work, growing old.

Jarre's first language was German, which she spoke at home and at school in Riga. She learned Italian when she moved to Italy, and although it became her language, the language she chose to write in, she still, she observed, "always had doubts about spelling and syntax," and "was limited [. . .] by a lack of inner connection to the technical means of the language." In an interview years later she said, "I envy Italian writers because Italian is their language." Tellingly, it was in German that she discovered what makes good writing.

The book's first section describes Jarre growing up in Latvia through a series of images, anecdotes, and sensations that create a picture of childhood and establish the outlines of family relationships. Time—a recurrent theme—generally goes forward in this memoir, but not in a straight line. The language can be allusive, and we often don't know where we are: we gradually find out as details accumulate. For example, throughout the first section there are references to the move to Italy, but we don't really have the whole story until we get to the end of the section. At the same time images are vivid and precise: taken to visit a newborn, Jarre says: "There's a smell of hot chocolate. The infant has bare legs and feet. He's fat and pale. Everyone says 'What a pretty baby,' but I feel like throwing up, maybe because of the smell of hot choco-late, maybe because I saw a hair wrapped around the child's big toe." Images bleed into other images: this one, for exam-ple, leads her to describe the foods she doesn't like as a child, the things that make her throw up, and then the foods she likes. This first section is narrated mainly in the present tense, the tense of a child's point of view.

The second section moves into the past tense. "Time entered my life," she writes of the move to Torre Pellice: she now has a past—that is, childhood. Significantly, along with time, history enters her life: not only her own but the past of her Waldensian ancestors. The Waldensians, a small Protestant minority in Catholic Italy, were concentrated mainly in the Alpine valleys of Piedmont, west of Turin; Torre Pellice was the main town in the area. The movement arose in France in the twelfth century, its followers joined the Reformation in the sixteenth, and over the centuries they were persecuted, suppressed, and often forced into exile. In Italy the Waldensians preserved many elements of their French culture, including the language. Thus when Jarre is taken to live in Italy she abruptly abandons the German of Riga not only for Italian but for French as well, the language she will speak at home with her grandmother.

The change from German to Italian and from Latvia to Italy is encapsulated in the story of the *Römer*: as a child in Latvia Jarre reads a book about the first-century general Arminius, who led the Germans in the battle of the Teutoburg forest against the wicked Römer, whom she doesn't recognize as the Romans, in fact or in name, until years later, when, reading a Roman history book in German, she realizes that she is now on the other side.

The second section has, so to speak, a French accent, and French appears regularly in the writing. These are the years of adolescence, and, just as the first section reflects the child's point of view here is the adolescent's: obsessive, dramatic, intense, self-absorbed, self-analytical, seeking to define an elusive self. Of a hike in the mountains with friends she writes: "Violent thoughts agitated me during the hike and sometimes became emotions: arriving among the first, descending among the last, talking to the boy I was in love with, but always life, with birth and death, and I, what was I doing there." At the same time, alternating with the adolescent dramas and descriptions of her own emotions are sharp and detailed pictures of her grandmother, of a hike in the mountains, of a substitute teacher, of collecting a prize for a winning essay at the local fascist headquarters. Here is history in many manifestations: history as the past to be studied or read about, history as family history (the herbs brought from Provence by her grandmother's mother), history as a lens through which to see the world, history as landscape, history as it is happening (these are the war years, and Torre Pellice was for a time occupied by the Germans), religious history.

The third section is in essence about the struggle to become an adult and a woman, to acquire and solidify an identity. It begins with Jarre imagining her own death, followed by thoughts on growing old and the way emotions diminish in intensity as one ages; she remembers learning to swim, thinks about being a woman, about her daughter and the inheritance of traits. Again we're in a space where past and future, real life, fantasy, and dreams mingle. Finally, reflecting on her daughter (now a mother herself), she asks the question, "What was I like as a young woman?" Now we're in a world of marriage, pregnancy, children, housework, a job as a French teacher. She also starts publishing, first stories, then novels, and finally a work about herself (that will become *Distant Fathers*). In this section the point of view changes again: we're still mostly in the past tense, but the tone is more detached and slightly ironic.

Jarre powerfully inhabits each point of view: the child, the adolescent, the woman striving to become herself. Within each she composes sentences that are like poems ("The cities I arrive in and depart from are always a station; as the train passes, mountains, rivers, plains become anonymous, and down there behind the lighted windows you see others in their precarious and illusory immobility, for they, too, are on the train traveling with me"); she can be graphic ("I have disgusting holes that stinky liquids come out of"); she's not afraid to present herself as unlikable or insensitive ("When they [the parents of a baby who died] left, they entrusted me with some money that had been collected for the upkeep of the grave. I let days pass and, in the end, negligently spent the money on myself").

In fact, Jarre is often an unlikable narrator; and certainly an unpredictable one, from the allusive, imagistic sentence that could be going anywhere, to the small, precise detail of a place or object, to a statement of fact: "I narrate." That narrative comes to us through a sensibility that is acutely self-aware, interrogatory, analytical, unsparing of herself and others. Jarre worked on this book for many years, and even when she got to the end she did not, as we see in the last line, resign herself to its truly being finished: there is always another layer to examine, always another way of looking.

The first section of *Distant Fathers* is dedicated to Jarre's younger sister, Annalisa, called Sisi (1926–87). The second is dedicated to Cecilia Kin (1905–92), a Russian writer and literary critic, who was known especially as a scholar of Italian politics and a literary translator from Italian. She was a friend of Jarre's, and among the first critics outside Italy to recognize her. The third part is dedicated to another friend, Lalla Gay (1934–2018).

I would like to thank Marta Barone, who is currently overseeing the reissue of Jarre's works for the Italian publishing house Bompiani, and the author's sons, Pietro, Paolo, and Andrea Jarre, for their help and, especially, for their invaluable reading of the translation.

Ann Goldstein

"A Stubborn Distance"

By Marta Barone

Marina Jarre is a great and lingering mystery. Why have her extraordinary novels and her unique voice, cool and searching yet ironic, tender, brutal, and astonishingly attentive to life and its details—why has all this, all together, not endured? Why isn't she considered, except by a few enthusiasts, to be among the great Italian writers of the second half of the twentieth century? Chance; bad luck (in a letter to a friend she complained with her usual irony, but also a slight weariness, about always writing the wrong thing at the wrong time: short stories when they weren't fashionable, "traditional" novels when experimentation dominated the literary scene, autobiographical writings when they interested no one); the "harsh reserve," noted by Claudio Magris in a 2015 article in *Corriere della Sera*, which led her to stay aloof, far from literary circles and worldly elites, to avoid presentations and everything that did not have to do directly with writing and the struggle to write—which was what uniquely interested her as an author. Whatever the reason for the silence that has enveloped her, maybe it's time to sweep away the dust and give Marina Jarre, who died in 2016 at the age of ninety, her rightful place in Italian literature.

Distant Fathers, originally published by Einaudi in 1987, comes in the middle of her career, and is probably her masterpiece. It was written almost without hope of publication, over the course of many years, and was revised continually, up to a masterly shine, words and phrases polished like pebbles in a high mountain stream: in letters she often speaks of a game of shifting scenes and chapters, like papers thrown into disarray so that she could find the right place for them, the best light. She called it "my autobiography," but like all the greatest books it goes beyond conventions and labels, breaks them down, and is primarily an intense investigation of identity; it's a work that re-creates the past by proceeding in a tight montage of often discrete images, which at the end, as in Nabokov's *Speak, Memory* or many of the novels of Annie Ernaux, form a stunningly comprehensive, organic portrait.

As if she were placing before the reader the glass plates of a magic lantern, Jarre begins to recount her life, which was certainly unusual, through patches of light cast here and there on various moments of her childhood, moving continuously and with supple grace between verb tenses (from the present to the past and from the past to the present) and between events, which she mixes up, anticipates, and suddenly returns to many pages later. Thus times and places, like the images of the labyrinth and the ocean in the poetry of the mysterious Alexia Mitchell, Cristina Campo writes, "seem to enter continuously into one another, and, equally fluid and sculptured, present the inextricable enigma of today and forever, of the labile and the permanent." [1]

---

1 Cristina Campo (1923–1977), Sotto falso nome (Under a false name): Milan (Adelphi, 1998). Alexia Mitchell was a pseudonymous poet whose identity was never discovered. (All notes are the translator's.)

Marina, nicknamed Miki, was born in 1925, in Riga, Latvia, the daughter of Samuel Gersoni, a Latvian Jew, and Clara Coïsson, an Italian, and a teacher at the university, who came from the Waldensian valleys of Piedmont, and was a prominent translator from the Russian for Einaudi (she translated among others Propp, Bulgakov, Tolstoy, and Dostoevsky). The childhood language of Marina Gersoni—who married Giovanni Jarre after the Second World War—was German: which is why her Italian often moves in an uncertain space that we've chosen to preserve, with its small peculiar "mistakes," with an effortfulness and an awkwardness that she had to deal with all her life, and which at the same time give her prose a strange magic, the unreality and intensity of a half language.

Marina the child is an observer with precocious awareness of herself and the space around her. She observes adults and their often senseless and melodramatic behavior: "Adults aren't afraid, that's the difference between them and me. I don't know if they're right not to be afraid: they walk on the ice on the lakes. The ice creaks; who can assure them it won't break?" She observes, without ever really knowing him, her absent father, reckless and cheerfully irresponsible, handsome as an "Arab prince," who stays out all night and by day goes around the house in dressing gown and slippers, smoking cigars with a gold band. She observes herself: in old age Jarre the writer reports with astonishing precision, at a distance of sixty years, the strange, incomprehensible, and also fierce feelings of childhood, jealousy of her younger sister, Sisi, shame ("I feel irrational tremors inside me, and I notice them with amazement. Certainly, they're not normal instincts, but so what . . . the important thing is for no one to know"), her relationship with her own body, the painful sense of inadequacy she feels in relation to her mother, who for Marina as a child and an adolescent represents reason and courage, but also unjust punishment, derision at her failures, and an increasing rage, making her silent and desperate because powerless (all children are powerless in the face of adults). What is the rage of a child? This, says Jarre:

> In front of me the icy sea expands to the horizon, spreading with its undulating motion. So white and full of frozen hollows it seems more impassible than in summer when the ships go by, even if they tell me that the Finns came as far as Riga in certain very cold winters, gliding over the sea in their sleds. It's immobile, but I know that it's seething underneath, that it wants to come out like the Düna in spring when it cracks its blanket of ice, and at night I hear it flowing with the sound of thunder.

Living in a mixture of nationalities in multicultural Riga, Marina knows that identities remain untouchable, even though she prefers "unnamed names—like the sound of the piano and the held breath of the winter wind when it's about to hurl itself, whirling, across the snowy plain," which "attract me, submerge me in a secret expectation, more than the named names, which you always have to think about precisely." The named names are many, and "you have to know them all and keep them in order and never lose them." She, "so they told me," is Latvian and Christian, even though "I speak German and I don't understand who Jesus Christ is." Her grandparents on her father's side, the grandfather Latvian and the grandmother Russian, are Jews. Her Italian grandparents are Waldensian, and also part French. Her mother is Waldensian. Her father would be Jewish, but has no religion. In her family Catholics are considered stupid, and no one explains to her the difference between Jews and Christians: "They're names I have to accept as they are." Maybe that's why, as an adult, Marina Jarre digs into names and words so diligently, trying to bring to the surface the mystery, the freedom, and the many meanings, aiming always at a precision that is different from cliché (or, as the French say, the *idée reçue*, the received idea, which gives an even better sense of her discussion of the names, or labels, that are imposed on her without explanation).

In 1935, after her parents' divorce, Marina and her sister are separated from their father and sent by their mother to live with their grandmother in Torre Pellice in northern Italy. Here, upon her arrival in the Waldensian valleys, a world that contains a tragic history of the persecutions and battles of distant fathers, proud, grim ancestors who, until almost a century earlier, had fought in the valleys to maintain their independence, a harsh world, where even places "carried time within themselves"—it's at this point, says Jarre, that "time entered my life." Time, one of the book's most important subjects, connects its parts into a constellation: "It gave me for the first time a past, a thickness in which to be submerged, avoiding investigations and assaults; the story of my childhood was what remained to me of my preceding existence, since in the space of a few weeks I changed country, language, and family circle." So begins Marina's long battle with Italian, which she's never spoken or written before.

The terrible fate of her father (he was killed in 1941, along with the rest of his family, including a child he'd had with a German nurse, in the extermination of the Jews of Riga) is just touched on in this book, as if Jarre were retreating from history and from her own story. Only much later did she decide to reckon with it, in *Return to Latvia* (published in 2003), which is in a way the completion of this book.

Jarre therefore continues to observe. She portrays the Waldensian world; the tremendous God of her mother's forebears, to whom she adapts poorly; her adolescence; fights with her grandmother; the slow separation from her sister, Sisi, at two different moments of growing up; friendships; and first loves. There is also the longing for her mother, who works abroad and whom she rarely sees, a longing that is never called by its name, but when she is speaking of the letters that she and Sisi wrote to her, an image from the future suddenly breaks in: "I was twenty when, going into my mother's room one day, I saw a letter on the desk, complete with salutation and signature, written in her beautiful clear handwriting. Even now the sight of any sample of her writing moves me, as if I had a more intimate relation with her writing than with her." This relationship of love, hatred, need, mutual incomprehension, jealousy, and unshakable loyalty lasted all her mother's life.

Fascism barely penetrates the valleys, apart from school ceremonies, and Marina barely perceives it, except that she is fascinated by ceremonies and eager to be like others, or in fact better than others—but she always gets something wrong and feels constantly deficient.

Something else arrives in her life at this moment, however:

I remember clearly when I realized that words placed in a certain order—following an absolute necessity— were beautiful. Rereading Schiller's *Don Carlos* yet again (I read and reread the books that affected me, I carried them with me everywhere, I didn't care about the name of the author and savagely skipped the pages that didn't interest me)—anyway, reading *Don Carlos* again, in the school edition that my mother, studying to be a teacher, had used at the university, I came to where the prince sees Elisabeth for the last time and says to her, *"So sehen wir uns wieder"* (so we meet again). I repeated the phrase and was moved. I heard a small pause after the *So* and the lengthening toward death of the final *wieder*. I was moved not because the prince was about to die—a standard occurrence in a play—but by the inevitability with which the words were joined together and separated, *those* words and in *that* way.

Jarre still doesn't know it, but she has discovered her fate, even though she didn't really begin to write until many years later, in Turin, already married and pregnant with her first child.

The war unfolds at a distance, unreal. She doesn't understand it and when finally it enters their lives she again finds herself observing, like a wary spectator, always tugged between very different impulses ("I found the whole thing incongruous, I couldn't see connections between events that didn't correspond to my usual readings of History, which corresponded, instead, to cheering crowds and orderly armies"). With the same implacability with which she dissected her childhood feelings and with which she explores those of the fictional characters in her novels, even the most unspeakable sentiments, the most obscenely natural, Jarre describes her uncertain, alienated, and hasty judgments about the war and, later, the resistance. She has a youthful arrogance and difficulty accepting that what was just and obligatory until a short time before has suddenly become wrong. She is overwhelmed by her incomprehension of events, by gestures previously inconceivable made by people she knows, including her grandmother, who on September 8th hides some deserters behind the clematis in the garden, has them strip off their uniforms, and gives them civilian clothes. She's very aware of her own uselessness: "I was generally a prudent girl, uninvolved and often cowardly."

She is always stopped on a threshold, she writes, even when some of her friends become partisans and one of them dies. Marina encounters a teacher, Franchi, who she knows is an antifascist; he comes up from the town staggering and asks if she knows that her friend was killed. Only later "an intuition slowly began to take shape in me: Franchi wasn't drunk; he was swaying because he was desperate. He was reproaching himself because it was his own teaching that had led Sergio to his death . . . But . . . I felt again a kind of respect. In that staggering I glimpsed, in fact, the despair of true pity, what was still denied to me, since I continued to feel compassion only for those with whom I could identify." Marina interrogates her inability to feel pity, her strange detachment, even when she decides to take part in some partisan activities as a courier; but "rage boiled inside me when, in a tram detoured deliberately, I passed the men hanged on Corso Vinzaglio; the violence was the greater the more impotent I felt, provoked that time even more by the dirty posters dangling above the hanged men than by the sight of their waxy doll-like faces."

Only the cry of a boy hanged in revenge at the end of the war by the fleeing Germans, a cry in the night, a cry to his mother, finally breaks the dissociation that inhabits her and opens her to "true pity." When a friend tells her about it, "I suddenly started crying, but the tears that bathed my face came not from my books and fantasies or, even farther back, from my petrified childhood, they flowed from my body, which was aware of itself for the first time, and in which I would have liked to hide and protect the unknown boy."

Of her Latvian childhood nothing remains except the rosy mirage of a long Baltic beach where she and Sisi gather shells and pebbles; they learn of their father's fate only ten years after the fact, and, like his person, and his frightening immensity, it falls into silence and repression. Yet Jarre writes, "his death remained within my life like a hidden seed, and gradually, as I lived and aged, it grew in my memory, not unlike a longtime love."

The third section is about herself as a woman: with her detached gaze, sometimes alienating and often permeated by a subtle, delightful humor, full of observations and surprising reflections. Jarre first of all describes her own old age, the changes in her imagination, her intelligence, her dream activity, and her desires, her daily routine (her writing here is among the best and most interesting in Italian literature on the old age of women; there are equally unforgettable passages in *Silence in Moscow*, written later, when she was much older, and perhaps more brutal as death approached). Then, with the same wavelike movement of the first part, she turns back, to herself as a young bride, to the possession of her own body only at the moment of becoming a mother ("As a woman I had to be born from myself, I gave birth to myself along with my children"), to the struggles of her years as a housewife, a French teacher in a school on the outskirts of Turin, a mother of four children, a wife, and, finally, a writer, though she gives only a few hints of what will become her true subterranean life: "the need to transform, the impulse to represent, to re-create, the conviction that everything can be reproduced and portrayed. Not in a tapestry with threads of silk and gold: my unicorn is still always a stray dog sleeping in the July heat in the cool shadow of a closed newsstand."

Yes, she is an extremely refined stray dog, and this is the other great theme of *Distant Fathers*: the lack of belonging, of homeland, of identity, at times proudly pursued, at times suffered, at times merely recorded as a fact. She feels a similar alienation from the Waldensian world, although it's partly hers: "There was no bond between me and that world, which remained outside me. No, the poor, rocky houses in shadow, the four pointed crests, the woman with the high, clear voice marked by those *r*'s were not related to me. Their history didn't precede me, I hadn't come from that." Just like the distance-closeness to her mother and to her own origins, contained in the image of the newly hatched ducklings who follow the cart in which the children are leaving the forest where they've been hidden from their father, leaving their childhood, and the lifelong avoidance of an anguished, irreparable, and annulled suffering. *Return to Latvia* was written, years later, to repair that mutilation at least in part.

Distant Fathers is a book of stone and splendors. Marina Jarre isn't a metaphysical writer, she never gives in to shouting and excess ("I don't weep and I am not amazed, I report"): her prose remains lean, smooth, and beautiful even in moments of great intensity, and maybe that's why her moments of lyricism, her magnificent metaphors, the incredible intuitions in her penetrating study of the mind of the living erupt on the page with such emotion and vividness, grand as a spectacle of nature, like the ice breaking up on the Düna. *Distant*

Fathers, so indefinable and original, so like its proud author, is something that was completely missing from the Italian literary landscape of the time, and which unknowingly prefigured the autofictional writing of recent years and the new directions it is taking. It's a book that still has much to say about writing and about human beings in the present and future, as great books always do. They keep going, and they keep us going.

The Circle of Light

For my sister Sisi

There are days when the sky above Turin is immense. Days of summer haze when from early morning the heat blurs the horizon, blurs on one side the hills and on the other the mountains. At dawn the trees rustle in vast leafy waves with a slow, continuous movement that spreads through the whole city. The sky looms opaque, a uniform yellowish gray, cloudless and still. Under this sky the swallows wheel and warble. Soon afterward, around eight, the trees, swaying more and more slowly, close in on the birdsong until their movement stops, the sky turns a violent yellow, and the sound of cars fills the streets.

I happen to hear Gianni and some of his friends talking about the Turin of their childhood and adolescence, when they'd go skating at the Italia: here was the footbridge over the railway; there they'd walk along the street with the brothels or on Via Roma before the reconstruction, when the buildings were still slanting over the old shops. Turin ended at the Mauriziano hospital, and there the fields began.

Talking about that Turin, Gianni and his friends aren't at all sad, aren't regretful about anything. I heard Gianni regretting only the tracks of the No. 8 tram that were torn up some years ago. "They'll see," he said, vengefully, "when

1

there's no more gas!" Once, walking through the Valentino park, he mourned the giant monkey puzzle tree in the botanical garden, whose stump, an enormous gray ruin, sticks out through the railings.

He talks about people, and as he talks the city narrows into a tight circle where everyone knows everyone else.

"She was bowlegged even as a child," he reflects, of a woman passing by.

"You know her?"

"No, but we were at elementary school together—she also went to Silvio Pellico."

He doesn't mourn the Turin of long ago, I say to myself, because he hasn't lost it. He hasn't lost his childhood.

I often envy other people's childhoods. Sometimes all of a sudden I'll envy a child in a stroller or a young pregnant woman with her trim, graceful potbelly. Envy flourishes in the unease I've always felt, at having to find out, at being excluded, and in the nostalgia I feel for the Turin of long ago that the child in the stroller and the slender young woman with her nice little belly come from, unchanged.

The regret that Gianni and his friends don't seem to feel feeds on what I don't know and haven't seen, on smells I haven't smelled, on the existence of that other I was not.

I've been in Turin for more than thirty years, and I know the new city that opened up like a ring around the old core thoroughly. It matured and aged with me, in its enormous avenues to the south and west bordered without interruption by large apartment buildings, in the new villas of the residential areas on the hill, in those foggy and less built-up neighborhoods near the highway to Milan, where on the street gas stations seem to predominate, and above, sparkling in the night, advertising billboards.

I spent a summer in Turin with a botanical book. At five in the afternoon I'd go out and walk along the perimeter of the gardens in the center and in the Crocetta neighborhood, or wander through the public parks, and I'd identify the trees by comparing them with the descriptions and illustrations in the book.

The summer wind lifted dusty scraps of paper toward the thick canopy of the horse chestnuts. In the park nearby, a Japanese pagoda tree flowered, while in the small garden on Via Bertolotti the acacia flowers were fading. In the Lamarmora Gardens the leaves of the Judas trees, in certain sunsets made bluish by the summer storms that swirl continually around the city, like black gates that open and close, sometimes to the north, sometimes to the south—the leaves of the Judas trees, as I was saying, were an intense pale green, lit by azure.

Looking around—would that be a wingnut or an ailanthus?—I'd be startled by a sense of solidarity, unspecified, undirected, yet addressed to those who, like me, were walking the streets of Turin in summer.

As I passed through neighborhoods, street after street, on dusty sidewalks littered with paper, squashed gelatos, condoms, syringes, dog poop, the street in the end became the place, the only one possible, indistinguishable from other places, and the people, and I with them on the sidewalk, indistinguishable from one another.

Large apartment buildings sprang up on interminable, empty, new, muddy boulevards, fragile at first in their spaced-out solitude, then settled within circles of earth planted with slender saplings—nettle trees?—or, unexpectedly, straight rows of maples furrowed the big parking lot between San Giovanni Vecchio and the Stock Exchange building: random changes, susceptible to further, daring transformations, made by an invisible hand in a single night. Debatable were the telephone booths, exact copies of the time- or space-travel machines in science fiction films, but obviously telephone booths—these, too, testifying to the daily need for, the naturalness of, such travels.

This is the place without a name, the same as other places, and my time the same as others' time. I will no longer escape.

When, as a child, I imagined running away from home, Italy was the country I would have liked to escape to. Italy, my mother's native country, where it was always warm and you spent long hours in the garden. So what if my summer vacations came with diarrhea, because of too much fruit picked unripe off the trees?

My sister and I were born in Riga.

A photograph of me at five: hair tied in two thick pigtails next to my tiny face, I'm standing, in a pretty striped velvet dress, chosen like the others by my mother, with a pinafore over it, beside the dollhouse, one hand on the flat roof, holding my doll Willi, who is next to the cage of Pippo the canary.

I have a hint of a gentle, stubborn smile and I'm gazing into the distance, sideways.

In another photograph, I'm looking away again, with the same half smile above the small obstinate chin, sitting next to my mother and my sister, who's looking straight ahead with shining, curious eyes. My mother, in profile, turned toward me, smiles a proud, emotional smile. She has two tiny wrinkles at the corners of her eyes.

My self-consciousness was tied to my fears, my awareness of others to my sister's appearance in my life.

We're going to the Kaisergarten. I walk with my hands resting on the bars of the carriage with my sister in it. I think I'm pushing it, and I remember distinctly the glint of the bars at the height of my head. Behind me walks the *Schwester*—naturally she's the one pushing the carriage. But I think: "Now they'll see me, they'll say what a good girl she is, taking her little sister out for a walk." We meet someone and stop. And that someone, up above me, says: "What eyes this child has, they really look like two black plums." I know right away that my sister's eyes look like black plums. The word "plum" has a very tender sound in German. And that same sound is repeated by my mother, when, later, the *Schwester* tells her the story.

At night I dream of walking on the maple leaves on that same sidewalk; next to me walks a tiny, soft, whitish being. I crush it, and crushing it gives me an immense sensation of power. I know that it's "alive" and that I can kill it. That it's at my disposal. Another time I find a lot of them on a low wall, and again I crush them. There's a large stain where I crushed them. Awake, I'm frightened by these dreams: awake, I can't hurt anyone, I can't even look at the coachmen who whip the horses. They've told me you have to kill a horse that falls and breaks its leg, because "if a horse falls it can't get up again."

I couldn't have been much more than two when we walked to the Kaisergarten, because there's only thirteen months' difference between my sister and me. From these thirteen months there are two photos in our family album. In the first, taken by my uncle, I'm sitting naked on a wicker chair in the sun, in the garden in Torre Pellice, in front of my maternal grandparents' house. My whole face is convulsed in laughter, and my mother, behind the chair, leans over me, smiling. In the other, taken by a photographer, I'm standing, propped against my mother, who is kneeling, in a very loose-fitting dress. I have a small, serious face, small eyes, a small nose, and a small mouth, sparse smooth hair. On the back of the photograph my mother has written something, referring to me as Marinette. I have no memory of that pretty name. When I was little I was called Miki—a nickname given to me by my sister—and my maternal grandmother called me Mina, accentuating the final *a* in the French way.

Maybe my love for the naked sun of fall and spring, when it seems to shine more brightly and boldly behind the trunks and the bare branches, belongs to the thirteen months that separate my birth from my sister's. Then every time memories of events not lived or feelings not consciously felt try to take shape in me, I say: "That's fine, I'm not afraid." Or I say: "I am the way I am, and I want to enjoy it."

But mostly I seem to be somewhere else, taking someone else's first steps.

On the other hand I knew very early on where I was, even if my awareness was limited to place and time—my room, our street, the edge of the beach brushed by the sea—and ignorant of movements. In that place and that time, any gesture or word of mine was very important, decisive. I fixed events in a frame where I could immediately confront them—at first everything seemed frightening—and I was unaware that one could wait or postpone.

So I had many fears—I was a coward, my mother said—in which people and places got confused: there were people who led me into difficult situations, places that evoked fearful presences. In every place and in every moment, however, I looked for the means, the act, or the word to resolve my fears by myself. I was also a liar, my mother said.

I'm afraid of my mother, I'm afraid of her when she's there, but I want her when she's not there. They tell me that's the love that *all* children feel for their mother. And their mother loves them because she suffered bringing them into the world. That I don't understand, why she loves them because she suffered. But I understand very well why the mother makes children, and that she has to have her belly cut open in the hospital to let them out.

When I was born, too, my mother went to the hospital. For weeks and weeks before I was born she vomited; she

7

would stop behind a fence to vomit in peace. She stopped vomiting the night before I was born. I was born several weeks early. That should finally give me some points, but it doesn't, because it was my mother who made me come out early, climbing up on a ladder to arrange some jars of jam in a cupboard.

Then I always had green poop and I cried at night.

I walked late and talked late; I seemed like an idiot, but the old *njanja* who played with me and sang me Russian songs when I woke up at night said I was very intelligent.

Adults aren't afraid, that's the difference between them and me. I don't know if they're right not to be afraid: they walk on the ice on the lakes. The ice creaks; who can assure them it won't break?

They leave stoves lighted at night, which then burn down their houses—especially the workers' houses on the outskirts—and the firemen have to rush to put out the fires.

My uncle throws me up and catches me midair. He's enjoying himself, but can he really catch me?

And finally, didn't the adults let even the Zeppelin fall, which one morning, all silvery in the sun, had passed right in front of our windows, facing the river Düna?

I, too, will become an adult, but I can't picture it to myself. It worries me—and I think about it often—that I will grow up suddenly, in a single night. How will I manage to find clothes the correct length right away, the next day? I'll have to go and buy them myself, and the adults will make fun of me because I'm wearing child's clothes that are too short.

They'll gladly make fun of me, and I hate being made fun of. In fact I hate anyone who makes fun of me.

Walking, I turn around to look at the street we've taken so that I can return home by myself if I'm abandoned. Similarly, in case my mother doesn't manage to get back on the train in time, I learn by heart the names of all the stations we pass through on the long, four-day journey that takes us to Italy in the summer: to Italy, to Torre Pellice. The first Italian name I learn is Garda, Lake Garda, and I see it through the train window just as I wake up one morning, a narrow strip of emerald-green water.

When I explain to my mother what I'm doing on the street, why I keep turning around during our walks, she's very offended.

But all I want is for her, finally, to praise me. Usually I let myself be carried from place to place like a package, and as soon as I arrive I hastily dig myself a den. I hate children's parties where some adult disturbs me in my corner, offering me enormous, disgusting slices of a creamy cake and asking questions about what I like. Do you like sledding, or skating? Do you like chocolate? Do you like going to nursery school?

Once, I'm taken to see a small baby, a newborn; we're in the house of someone from the Dutch legation. I've found a sheltered place behind a big curtain, next to a window, and I'm looking at an illustrated book, reading the captions in capital letters. And here's the usual adult flushing me out and taking me with the other children to see the newborn. The room with the cradle is brightly lit and full of people. There's a smell of hot chocolate. The infant has bare legs and feet. He's fat and pale. Everyone says "What a pretty baby," but I feel like throwing up, maybe because of the smell of hot chocolate, maybe because I saw a hair wrapped around the child's big toe.

Every so often I throw up. I don't like eating meat, and I can hold pellets of chewed meat, carefully placed in the corners of my mouth, unswallowed, for a whole afternoon. When my mother digs them out with her finger, she scolds me. She's right, I ought to swallow them; if I don't, I won't grow.

When I had whooping cough, she got oranges through the Italian legation. They cost a lot and are lined up on a high shelf. I eat them to make her happy, then throw up—expensive as they are—while my sister, who has whooping cough as well, manages to keep them down. My mother tells the story and laughs as she describes my sister, who quickly coughs, swallows again, and returns to her game, saying: "Done!"

I don't like eating; there are only a few foods I really love. Salmon, boiled or smoked. At night I go looking for it in the dark, pink and fragrant on the kitchen table, ready for the next day. I also like eating kissel (a sour berry dessert) and spaghettini in broth, and even würstel: we buy them in the German stations on our trips, served on a cardboard tray with mustard and a white roll. But all these foods have features unrelated to their taste that appeal to me: the beautiful pink of the salmon or the jellylike transparency of the kissel, the steamy smell of the würstel and the elegant shape of the white roll.

On the other hand I don't find cod-liver oil disgusting. There's nothing food-like about it, in fact; it's more like liquid glue. While my sister hides under the table and behind the sofa when the moment for the daily dose arrives, I sip it dutifully. Naturally I hope by this means to finally get some points, though the truth is it doesn't cost me much. But perhaps my mother divines my repulsive dietary instincts; she seems almost disgusted by my obedience toward the cod-liver oil, sympathizing with my sister, if with a severe expression, as she drags her out from behind the sofa. What would she say if she knew that, shut in the bathroom, I regularly eat Nivea cream, then carefully lick the surface smooth?

Every so often I have the impulse to tell her that I eat the Nivea cream in the bathroom; but what if instead of scolding me she started laughing? Or I'd like to tell her why I stay so long in the small toilet off the kitchen. They're always getting mad at me because I often sit in there, and to think that I'm not disturbing anyone; sitting on the toilet lid, I talk to the dog shut up in the lightbulb.

Actually shut up inside the filament, and I talk to him, I feel sorry for him and I feel sorry for myself: "Dog," I say to him, "you're there, shut up, and I'm here, shut up, and when I come out they scold me and tomorrow morning they'll give me a cold bath." Also, I've discovered that when I have a cold I smell a disgusting odor inside my nose. "Dog, you don't have a cold; you're clean, odorless, and luminous in your filament."

But I don't talk to my mother. My lack of points paralyzes me. When she looks me in the face, I feel that she's looking into my depths. Useless to pretend, I'm worth nothing. If they'd at least feel sorry for me, but no one feels sorry for me. They don't even feel sorry for me when I'm sick. I'm often sick, with stupid illnesses that are called "childhood." When my sister was a few months old, she was so seriously ill she was in danger of dying. Then she was never sick again.

My mother recites my stupid illnesses like the rosary of her suffering; she worries when I get sick and stays home to take care of me. When I start to get better, every temperature check is a critical moment. Once, when the thermometer still says 37.5, not 36.8, she gets so angry that she throws it up in the air. Or she throws something else up in the air, I don't remember what. "What did you do? Did you get up to go to the window? Did you not put on your slippers, did you jump on the bed?" I'm afraid of her, but I feel sorry for her: she's right, she has to stay home to take care of me when she has so much work at the university.

Whereas I am very happy to get sick. Precisely because she has to stay home to take care of me. Apart from the sticky yellow compresses for a sore throat and the spoon handle the doctor uses as a tongue depressor, I love all the ritual of illness. The pale soup in the bowl on the tray—the tray all for me, with a clean napkin—and, needless to say, the taste of the syrups. Every morning my mother washes me carefully and dusts me with talcum powder. Enveloped in the perfume of my ablutions, I stay in bed under the covers and watch the sun on the wallpaper. It, too, is all mine in its small square of light on the wall. I'm sheltered from every peril; I can rest from the labors of daily defense.

I'm curled up like a spider in the middle of my life, weaving a web of protection all around myself. I can never leave my post, and I depend on myself, I can't allow a moment's distraction: I release as little of myself as possible into the hands of the others who are trying to destroy me bit by bit.

With their questions, with their laughter: "Do you like to skate? Do you like going to nursery school, do you like chocolate?" Or: "Say this, say that, what do you say to the lady?"

Whatever I say, they laugh.

The efforts of my mother and grandfather to make me say *merci*, when Grandfather offered me a bunch of grapes under the hazelnut tree in the garden at Torre Pellice, were useless. My grandfather was—strangely—in his bathrobe. He was already very sick and spent most of the day in bed. That afternoon he had gone slowly out to the lawn to pick grapes. Now he was holding them in his hand, the beautiful gilded grapes, but I couldn't open my mouth. My grandfather pressed his lips together, impatient and disappointed.

A few months later we're back in Riga, and one morning our governess takes us to Mamma's room. She's sitting on the bed in her slip, her arms bare, and she's weeping, wrinkling her nose. Our grandfather in Italy has died.

This time, too, I was silent, out of prudence, certainly, so as not to compromise myself. But still I was surprised: I had never seen my mother cry, and I didn't understand why she was crying.

It didn't move me—adults didn't move me, our dying dog moved me, as he vainly gasped for air with his sick muzzle. Rather, it seemed to me that she was no longer my mother (she was Grandfather's daughter), and that made her so distant in her inexplicable emotion—weren't we, my sister and I, the sole object of her feelings?—that she could no longer be feared.

Besides, you're not supposed to make a show of your feelings, those who do are surely putting on an act.

The last time I saw my father—I was twelve, he and my mother were getting divorced, and he had come to see us for a few days in Torre Pellice, where we had been living with our grandmother for two years—we said goodbye in Vicolo Dagotti, the narrow street where my grandparents' house was. Maybe I was on the way to school; I was alone, probably my sister had left before me. Just as I was about to turn onto the main street, my father, who had been standing at the corner, hurried after me and, catching up, lifted me in his arms and kissed me, weeping, on the mouth. That gesture—so alien to the habits of our relationship—stunned and repulsed me. When he put me down, I ran away without saying goodbye and left him there, on the street, tall in his dark overcoat.

As I turned onto the main street, running, and wiped my mouth with my hand, I continued to wonder: What was he thinking? And at the same time I wondered: Who is he?

My surprise, however, was the opposite of the surprise provoked by my mother's crying. That had revealed her to me as alien, whereas my father's sudden and unusual gesture—not rehearsed—had aimed at holding on to something in me. Something that wasn't there, that was absent.

That absence I felt immediately as guilt, long before I knew that I had left him in Vicolo Dagotti for the last time, tall in his dark overcoat, erect before the Germans who shot him in Riga in October or November of 1941[2].

Guilt shared between him and me that we had been unable to know each other.

I know almost nothing about him. I have only scattered childhood memories. I don't know how he and my mother met, for a long time I didn't know why they got married. I don't know the date of his death. The date of his birth I dug up in the documents regarding the divorce between my mother and him.

Before leaving for the last time, he had given me a watch. It was big, with an irregular rectangular shape and Roman numerals that I really didn't like. Years before, he had given us a doll as tall as I was, which wouldn't fit in any doll bed. He gave us one doll each time, without saying which of us it was for; he had brought a Negro doll from the exposition in Paris that my sister immediately took, though certainly when he bought it my father didn't know who would get it. During one of the legally arranged visits he made in the last months we were in Latvia, he had given us—poor man— some immense white plush rabbits. Horrible, larger than life animals, which you couldn't play with.

---

2 The Germans occupied Riga in July of 1941. In late November and early December, most of the city's Jews were shot; among these were Jarre's father and his relatives, including a six-year-old daughter named Irene he had had with a German nurse.

He never sent me the dolls' tea set I kept asking for in all the letters I wrote from Torre Pellice; the porcelain tea set, a gift from my mother, remained in our house, along with the toys, my books, and my dolls. We'd had to leave without taking anything, pretending to go to school one morning; instead we had gone to Mamma in the house where she lived after the separation.

Every so often, even now, I dream that I have to pack my suitcase and can't take what I need. Generally I dream of having to flee with my small children and having to choose what clothes of theirs to take. I have to collect blankets, too, in a hurry, before the imminent catastrophe.

I wore the watch for a long time, and only many years after it broke did I decide to replace it with another, a very small one. I kept the large, cumbersome broken watch among my trinkets; then during a move I threw it away.

I kept nothing else having to do with my father, not a photograph or a letter. Not even the last letter he wrote us, in 1941, right after the Germans occupied Riga. I can't absolutely remember what happened to that letter, which for some years I kept among my papers; it was torn and creased, but I don't know by whom. My grandmother hated our father and would certainly have been capable of getting rid of any trace of him. But it's not impossible that it was I who threw away the letter in one of my cleaning operations.

Of that letter, written in his illegible handwriting, I recall only one sentence, which he had underlined: " . . . because, remember that you, too, are Jewish."

A phrase that I considered meaningless, as I couldn't in the least understand the reason he asked us—I was sixteen and my sister fifteen—to get him out of Latvia by any means. How could we ever have managed that?

There had been no intimacy between us: he was the only adult who not only didn't embody rules but, rather, rejected them all.

He lived like a stranger in our mother's large, light, and orderly house. He was tall, dark, bald at the temples—he was almost forty when I was born—and probably very handsome. He looked like an "Arab prince," said the cook.

Our day didn't coincide with his. Sometimes I ran into him when I went out in the morning to go to school on streets that were still dark, illuminated by streetlamps. He was coming in, a white silk scarf around his neck. When I got home at one I found him going through the rooms in slippers and bathrobe, with a terrible man's odor about him. Or he was sunk in an armchair, reading his Russian newspapers, smoking fat cigars with a gold band that for fun I put on my finger like a ring. At lunch he ate jellied calves' feet. He drank tea in a tall glass circled by a ring with a handle.

One afternoon he went with us to the ballet, instead of Mamma, and fell asleep at the back of the box. He snored so loudly that you could hear him in the orchestra.

Sometimes he took us to a sporting event. He was interested in sports and had been a coach in the Soviet Union. He said: "In 1918 I was in a boat on the Düna and they shot at me from the bridge." That was why he had had to flee to the Soviet Union.

I remember that when he told the story he imitated the whistling of the shots.

Once we went with him to a track meet. A dark little bowlegged man, all sweaty, was walking very fast around a circular track. He was gesturing, speaking an incomprehensible language, and when he was given a glass of water he sipped it and then spit it out. I felt embarrassed because he was Italian and my mother was also Italian, like that comical, rude little man.

My father disparaged the Italians and especially one of them—a certain Mussolini—who for a while I thought was also a track athlete. He disparaged the Soviets and the Germans as well. He tried to teach me a strange German—Yiddish—and was very amused when I pronounced it the way he did. Mamma got mad and said he had it in for the Germans because he couldn't finish the university in Germany.

But almost all his friends were German. "Worthless Germans," said Mamma. One was a prison doctor, and his wife had come to our house one afternoon to protest, because *Herr Gersoni* was always persuading her husband to stay out all night. My father was amused to be setting a bad example. But that other, a "worthless German," why did he agree?

Our father did other things that fathers don't do and shouldn't do.

Once he bought a bus. He took us to see it in the garage where it was parked.

The bus's seats were torn, and right away I wondered—but didn't dare ask for confirmation—if we would be driving around in that bus instead of in the Diatto. I'd already had to travel in a sidecar that wobbled on the pavement beside the motorcycle. But luckily the bus was only a "deal" of my father's. The Diatto was, too—in fact, for a while, two Diattos were—and perpetually awaiting a buyer.

My father's deals were those oddities—like his interest in sporting events—that occupied him instead of, Mamma said, his office. He was the Michelin representative for the Baltic countries.

My dreams of Riga are exclusively about the street where his office was located. In the dreams the street is empty, with a buckling pavement bordered by tall houses that lean toward the street all together like the tops of an avenue of poplars in a stormy wind. It's an anguished dream in which the pavement and the houses are black, and I'm running toward my father's office and I want to find him. But I find—sitting in a chair one after the other, in a succession of very quick changes—unknown men with old faces and closed eyes. I wake up crying.

On the way home after the visit to the bus, our father and mother fight.

They don't get along. It's his fault, he shouts loudly, but doesn't change his behavior. He doesn't display the least goodwill, and Mamma has to work hard to pay all the bills. He goes to Paris twice a year "to have fun."

They don't get along; they've never gotten along.

When I find an old postcard written by my mother in which she tells her parents that I'm sitting in the high chair, and I look at them, Sammi and her, while they have lunch, it seems to me she's talking about other people.

Their not getting along is a daily fact that my sister, Sisi, and I talk about every so often. How can one get along with someone who goes to Paris twice a year to have fun? Who sleeps during the day, doesn't pay the bills, and shouts? The cook says to the maid that he's hit Mamma, but that I don't believe; then when he starts shouting I'm afraid he will.

Mamma is very brave. She stands up to him when he yells. She stands up to everyone, even the customs officials. While they rummage in our suitcases, she insults them.

One spring morning we have to move. Every so often we move: the first house I remember was on the Düna, and from the windows we could see boats passing; then we lived on the other side of the river, and there was gym equipment hanging in the doorway between the dining room and the study. In another house, they let me arrange my doll furniture at the end of a small dead-end hallway. The apartments were always very large, and every room had a different smell.

That spring morning we drive with our father and mother to Bienenhof, the property belonging to our grandfather on an island in the Düna. Besides the factory there's also the house where our grandparents lived, along with our father and his first wife, before they came to Riga.

Our father has proposed going to live in Bienenhof and Mamma is pleased; she likes the idea. I don't remember anything about the trip except that my father and mother get along.

It's a sunny day, and the whole house is in the sun when we arrive. In front of the house is a giant white lilac that— our father recounts—was split by a grenade during the war and continued to bloom from the two trunks that grew out of the divide. My father lets me touch the trunk.

Then we go to the house. The apartment is on the first floor. The windows are open and the sun lights up the rooms. The furniture is old and pale, and white dust covers sheathe the chairs. The floors are of waxed blond wood. There are a lot of rooms. My father and mother go from room to room; I can't hear what they're saying but I know they're getting along.

I look out the window into the grassy courtyard. I'm hungry and I'd like a sandwich. I play my game of smells; I walk with my eyes closed, differentiating the smells of the various rooms I pass through.

The rooms in Bienenhof smell of sun, of dust covers, and naturally of honey. *Biene* in German is bee. They don't smell of people.

We didn't go to live in Bienenhof, and our father and mother divorced.

I don't think I hoped to go and live in Bienenhof. I didn't know the future, enclosed as I was in the lighted circle on my stage. My parents' divorce was in that circle every day, there with the other fears.

That morning in Bienenhof, the circle of light only expanded, expanded so that I could no longer see its edges, beyond the bright walls and out the open windows, beyond the grassy courtyard and the river that you crossed on a wooden bridge.

I played the game of smells for the last time in Waltershof, the property belonging to German aristocrats where my mother hid us during the last months we spent in Latvia. Our father and mother were getting divorced—the case lasted for six years—and Mamma intended to take us illegally to Italy, afraid that the court wouldn't give us to her. We were informed of all this by our governess Ingeborg—we called her Böggi—who had helped Mamma prepare for our flight and lived with us in Waltershof.

To get to our room in a wing of the building, you crossed living rooms and small sitting rooms full of cabinets with gilded legs and chairs enveloped in dust covers. In a corner room whose windows were always closed there was from midnight till one a headless ghost that was connected—I no longer remember how—to an eighteenth-century grandfather clock given by Marie Antoinette to a goddaughter, a forebear of the house's owner. I crossed that room with my eyes closed, sniffing the odor of ghost, a small, faint, gray smell that didn't reach my nose but only the remote den in my head where I huddled.

In this den I ceaselessly arrange what is happening.

I can only side with my mother; I've always sided with my mother. From her come all the rules, and she's the one I've been courting forever. Besides, she's the one who loves me. Does my father love me?

In the months spent in Waltershof I don't dream. My day follows me even into sleep; sometimes I wake up in the morning and I've wet the bed. The fact is made public, and a young man—a Polish aristocrat who is getting agricultural experience on the farm and courting our governess—composes a poem; transcribed in graceful handwriting and decorated with a frame of little violet flowers, it's read after lunch in front of everyone before being handed to me. I burst into tears, and he is bewildered and asks my pardon. But my suffering remains, so to speak, outside me. I don't even hate the young man, I'm too worried about putting things in order inside my head.

In the last days I was at home with my father I had to lie to him. Keep hidden from him our meeting with Mamma—the delicious odor of her fur rediscovered when she hugged me—and the arrangements made for joining her the morning of the last day of school before Christmas vacation. She was staying with friends very near our school, and we were supposed to enter the house by ourselves, go up the stairs, and tell the young man, the son of the owner, who would open the door, that we wanted Mamma. To allow him—I think—to testify that we had come of our own free will. I—who had been entrusted with the message—was so agitated I couldn't say a word.

I regret being silent with my father. While I play warily with my dolls in a room that's been turned upside down—we'd taken advantage of our mother's long absence to place our child's desks on top of each other, making them into

23

little houses—and my father eats jellied calves' feet, sitting in his bathrobe at the dining room table, I feel that I pity him. I know it's not reasonable, but pity hurts like a scratch that's festering under the Band-Aid. Even when I wake in the night, pity is there, and it wakes with me.

Sometimes—but only for very brief moments, from which my thought rises rapidly like a sparrow that, having thought it spied a crumb, rises from the ground without even touching down—it occurs to me to stay with my father.

I feel pity for my mother, too, but the pity I feel for her is right because my mother is right. And that rightness is set solidly in my head, with well-defined corners, as hard as a block of wood. It governs my steps and my hands, and governs my tongue, too, when we're summoned to declare before the lawyers whom we want to stay with, and I have to say in front of my father that I want to stay with Mamma. I say it and lunge forward, leaping blindly. The same blind leap with which I'll lunge forward whenever in the course of my life I have to choose her, what's right. Her, Mamma. Then I grope behind myself and can't get to myself. I'm not patient; besides, I find that I've already done enough by choosing her, what's right. I would like to be left in peace now with my dolls, my babies; I'd like to water the flowers, then go out at sunset and smell the summer fragrance of the hay far beyond the stony confines of the city. I'll come home late and cook for my children. For my father.

Our father had found us in Waltershof after searching throughout Latvia. Our governess tells us that he searched for us to get revenge on Mamma, because she left him. He arrived unexpectedly in the car, when we were playing in the courtyard. We had to escape quickly into the house and shut ourselves in our room. My father knocked on the door and called. He called me by name. He called me because I was a coward and maybe I would open the door to him. But I didn't, and in order to hold out I began to do calculations on a piece of paper: the numbers came out crooked because my hand was trembling. I watched it tremble and I was amazed because I wasn't making it tremble and it was trembling just the same.

Then my mother arrived—I heard her voice clearly behind the door—and we were called into that room to declare whom we wanted to live with.

My father isn't courageous. Only I know that one night he was awake in the living room, next to our bedroom, smoking. I was sitting behind the door watching through the keyhole the luminous tip of his cigar in the dark room. I sat on the floor until I got cold and too sleepy to keep it up and went back to bed. My father was awake because he was afraid: the next day he was going to the hospital to have an operation. My father is a coward like me. I feel sorry for him because he's a coward.

The night they told him on the phone—I don't know if it was the lawyer, who remained just a name, or Mamma—that she wasn't coming back, he began running through the rooms and looking out the windows, leaning his forehead against the glass. He leaned his forehead against the window and, looking into the street, cried, "I've lost you, Clarette, I've lost you forever!" That endearment I found ridiculous, unsuited to my mother.

My sister and I stayed shut in our room, but he also came to us and shouted, his forehead against the window that faced directly onto the street. After everything he had done to her—he had even hit her, certainly!—now he was making these scenes and lamenting that she didn't want him anymore.

Nevertheless I felt sorry for him, precisely because he was playing a part. He was playing himself, he had to shout so that they would believe him. And no one believed him.

And no one loved him. Not even I, who had to be loyal to my mother. I feel sorry for him because I don't love him.

I love my mother: she's the one who's always loved me and taken care of me.

I say: when I grow up I'll be a teacher like Mamma.

When she went out to the university, my father's office, the theater, a reception, in her wake wafted a breeze of cologne and soap. She not only teaches the rules but applies them all to herself. Naturally it takes effort and courage to apply the rules: the rules are harsh.

Before going out she moves back and forth through the house, checks on our food, our conversations, our notebooks, our clothes, she corrects a word, cautions the governess.

At Christmas, a few weeks after our flight, we're hidden in a castle at the edge of a big forest. Afterward, we would go to Waltershof.

Mamma has set up a tiny Christmas tree—at home the tree touched the ceiling—and under the tree, instead of the usual toys, we find the pajamas we need precisely because we fled without taking anything.

The candles throw a yellowish light on the uneven walls, where you can make out the rough shape of the stone under the paint. I ate too much pâté at Christmas lunch. I adore pâté. I feel a little sick to my stomach and I feel sorry for my mother who had to give us pajamas instead of toys. I feel sorry for her because she's brave.

I try to be loyal to her and apply the rules. But I'm not very smart about applying the rules and I often make mistakes. Behind the principal rule there are unstated rules, and if you can't get them right all together, the first goes wrong, too. Coming home and hurrying by, my mother scolds me.

My sister is much less assiduous than I am about observing the rules, but she seems to have understood precisely those other, unexpressed rules, which end up, I don't know how, being the most important.

Once my mother meets a Gypsy who tells her: "You have two daughters. I see one of the two on the stage. She'll bring you glory!"

My mother tells the story: "Sisi walks so well on point— look how well she walks on point—maybe she'll be a ballerina, or a singer. Hear how musically she sings."

I can't even skate. The skating rink where my sister flies, tracing beautiful figure eights, is one of the places I hate most:

I drag myself to the edge with my ankles collapsing, and I'm cold. The others have fun. Lucky them.

But skating is good for your health, sledding down steep hills is good, getting into freezing-cold water without complaining is good. Plus you have to do these things better than everybody else.

Once (we're already in Torre Pellice) my mother sends me in a letter a newspaper clipping with the photo of a classmate—one of those great big Germans my sister skated with—who'd won some competition. Under the photo she wrote: Look what Marlene was capable of!

All I know how to do is read, I read all day. But reading isn't a skill.

Years later—I'm married and my four children are born—we're all in the kitchen, my children, sitting at the table in their pajamas after their daily bath (first rule: be clean!), are waiting for me to finish making dinner. My mother, who has come to visit, as she does every evening, is telling my children about when, with my sister, I took the admissions test for middle school in Torre Pellice. We had learned Italian in eight months, and Sisi, a year younger than the required age, had to retake Italian and drawing in September. My mother says to my children: "They had to write a composition on the experience of elementary school, which Aunt Sisi and your mamma had attended only briefly. Miki, who was a liar, invented an entire story, Sisi, poor thing, who was so sincere, didn't know what to write."

Other times she tells about when I pooped on the seat

of a train; I was eleven months old, and she, pregnant with my sister, was traveling that time without a baby nurse. Or she tells about when, at only three, I pretended to have appendicitis.

One afternoon, my youngest son—he was six—comes home from his grandmother's house, where he'd gone for lunch, and asks me: "Mamma, why does Grandma always say bad things about you?"

Applying the rules is of no use to me, the unexpressed ones that my sister relies on elude me: she shifts easily from one situation to another, she dares to speak to the mailman in slightly incorrect Latvian—I would never have dared to speak to the mailman in Latvian, even slightly incorrectly—and walks down the hall at school arm in arm with other girls, giggling and eating *tartine*.

My sister is dark, I'm blond—my mother is very proud of my hair; when she washes it, she rinses it with chamomile—and Sisi has a pink silk dress (which I remember very well); I have one of blue silk, in the same style (which I don't remember at all).

My mother likes my hair, she combs it, brushes it, admires it. She doesn't praise anything particular about my sister, except that when Sisi and I are grown-up, I sometimes hear her praise my sister's beauty: "She looked so beautiful in that white suit."

What's beautiful makes my mother's voice tender.

We're in Italy now, I'm more than ten years old. When Mamma joins us during vacations, she takes us on short "cultural" trips. She knows Italy perfectly, the geography, the cities, the streets, the museums, the idioms of the various regions. (At the age of eighty, bent over by an attack of arthritis, she comes to the door as I'm leaving for Pisa and urges me not to forget to "say hello to Santa Maria della Spina, that little jewel.")

During one of our educational excursions we're in Genoa and, after visiting a museum, we take the tram. The tram goes up and down, pitches, I feel sick to my stomach, I'm about to throw up, we have to get off. My mother, furious, insults me: *"Krepierling!"* she says to me. "Jerk!" Her rolled *r* wounds me like a weapon, but above all I'm struck by the sensation of being restored to myself in my disgustingness: she doesn't want me, she's not the one who made me so wretched, it's my fault, I'm a freak of nature.

I didn't think Sisi was pretty or prettier than I was. I was told that Mamma was beautiful and very elegant. I was enchanted—and I still remember it—by the clarity of her face, and when we were separated I thought of her in that clarity.

I had a geometric idea of beauty; beauty is regularity. One day, in school, our homework assignment is to plan a design for a small tablecloth, and on a big sheet of graph paper—I adore graph paper and mathematics notebooks—I draw a square with a bouquet of flowers in the middle and four smaller bouquets, one in each corner. The colors, pink and green. Aren't flowers pink and leaves green? When I'm embroidering the tablecloth I find it hideous—the ugliest in the class—but I can't understand the reason.

For a long time all I liked were Doric columns, refectory tables, and Corneille.

Yet I remember as beautiful my blond *Fräulein Leni*—incomparably beautiful, more beautiful than anyone—while she read me stories and talked to me. One night I'm thrilled to suddenly hear again her sweet, secret German voice whispering timid, tender-sounding phrases in a documentary on television with commentary by Ulrike Meinhof.

Voice and language, you who respond to someone or something that calls to us within ourselves, and not to those who stand by and listen.

Maybe women are beautiful. A little girl is neither beautiful nor ugly. A little girl likely has flaws.

For example, I have disgusting holes that stinky liquids come out of. I don't care that adults probably have them, too, I never think about it. Just as I never think about that repulsive contraption—a glass cylinder with rubber tubes—that is hanging in the bathroom. I don't even want to look at it.

Once, when I was very small, Mamma gave me a terrible scolding because after my afternoon nap my hands smelled of pee. Pee is dirty, you have to do it, but don't touch it.

You mustn't touch yourself, and I had done some cleaning in that little hole I have between my legs. I like cleaning that little hole.

How beautiful the apple is, round, smooth, with a slightly sour smell. Passing a fruit and vegetable shop and seeing a box of apples, round, solid, perfect, without holes,

I have a sudden mad wish to bite one. I stop the governess and beg her to buy me an apple; I'm hungry, I say. We're not allowed to eat outside of meals, and she won't buy it for me.

In fact no one is really beautiful, not even adults. The apple is beautiful and the trees in the forest just after a snowfall. And the spiteful black-haired princess under the silver crescent moon is beautiful. She dances with the prince, they whirl from one side of the stage to the other. He lifts her up high with a rapid, light gesture. They're beautiful, smooth, without holes; they have stockings that cover them from neck to feet. I prefer the spiteful black-haired princess to that insipid blonde the prince has met beside the lake.

I feel irrational tremors inside me; sometimes I admire bad people and I want to be like them.

Besides, my mother also admires bad people, people who don't get outsmarted, who are stronger, who know how to talk back.

The bad are strong, so their lies are different from the lies of cowards.

My mother admires my sister when she manages to outsmart me. She says so, too, and laughs.

I take good care of my dolls: I comb their hair and dress them, I dust their furniture, make their beds, and wash plates and pots. I rock them to sleep and walk them in their carriage, a real carriage with a top. Sisi tears out the hair on hers and carries them around with arms and legs pulled off, she doesn't have a complete set of dishes, and she kicks the piano during lessons.

Mamma laughs when she looks at Sisi's dolls, and laughs even harder when she says: "Sisi has handed off her broken dolls to her sister, sending them 'to board' with her; she'll fix them."

And so she laughs when she reports that at night my sister "forces" me to tell stories until I fall asleep. Sisi doesn't sleep and says, "*Oof*, that idiot is asleep."

My mother reports to the others what I do.

In fact I'm happy to fix broken dolls, and happy to wash pots and happy to tell stories. I wouldn't do it if I didn't like it. I try to avoid what I don't like as much as possible. The trouble is that I like hardly anything. Maybe that's precisely what disgusts my mother.

Besides, the things I like I like secretly. They don't come under the rules. I can't talk about them.

I walk between the rows of covered stands at the Christmas market. There are a lot of colored lights; brightly lit on the stands are papier-mâché toys, hot *cialde*—their greasy fragrance spreads in the cold air—and embroidered fabrics. The venders at the stands talk in loud voices and the people passing by respond in loud voices.

I wouldn't want to have any of those toys—papier-mâché, imagine!—and even less eat the hot cialde. But I like walking amid those noisy, cheerful people. I'm one of them, nobody knows about my shameful secrets, and, seeing me pass by, they'll think I've just eaten a smoking-hot salami and am about to buy a wooden puppet.

I feel irrational tremors inside me, and I notice them

with amazement. Certainly, they're not normal instincts, but so what, I cultivate them cautiously, the important thing is for no one to know.

With a secret shiver I wait at the circus for the clowns to kick each other in their enormous soft fake bottoms, then walk away, loose-limbed, complaining in weak, artificial voices. I imagine that that rear end is real. I imagine that there's no rope pulling the row of swans along the back of the stage. Mamma boasts of how astute my sister is who sees that rope right away.

But I wish that the princess's silvery dress were of real silver. That behind the trees of the magic forest there were other trees and behind those trees castles and in the castles wizards. And I'd like to touch the bare white arms of the equestriennes just resting on the saddles of the black horses. Oh shapely white arms, I would have liked to touch them, or, rather, fondle them. And so I'd like to rest my hand in the place where I see the breasts start to separate. Right in that furrow.

And the little gold ring with the blue stone in the hole-in-the-wall shop: every day I looked at it and wanted it; I even had a plan ready to steal the money needed when one fine day it disappeared from the shop window.

I don't always succeed in hiding under my edifice of points; I construct it carefully, but then some terrible flaw jumps out as if from a filthy hole and I say and do something I shouldn't. And ruin everything. Yet I feel pleased: I'm not exactly proud of that terrible flaw, but, what can I say, I'm fond of it.

Then I'm sorry, but because of the consequences, not because I've said or done "that thing." I don't know why, but I also feel I'm right.

I reveal to my mother why I always turn around during our walks. And when I see that she's starting to get mad, I insist: She could abandon us and then how would we get home?

The doctor comes, I have a hard time sticking out my tongue, but I make an effort to go along with the whole ritual until he says "Cough." Then I lie down again. The doctor writes on his prescription pad, my mother is nervous, she's in a hurry. The doctor asks if by any chance I've worn a garment that irritated my skin, and I immediately report the new pajamas. My mother gives me a nasty look, but I'd like to get rid of the pajamas, which do make my skin itch. But I've spoiled things, this illness won't get me any advantage. Besides, it's not a serious illness. I never have serious illnesses. For instance: I get paratyphoid fever, I don't get typhoid.

Some pastries are missing from the tray and I tell on Sisi, who denies it though she still has a mustache of cream around her mouth. She tells lies, too, like everyone else, but since she doesn't care about telling them well, it's as if she hadn't told them.

Mamma has to punish Sisi and prepares to do it right away. Mamma is just and severe: if you make a mistake you have to pay. My sister licks off the cream mustache and goes on denying. Mamma grabs her by the arm and drags her screaming to the door: they'll take the rest of the pastries to the pastry shop to be weighed, and so my sister's sin will be evident. Halfway down the stairs Sisi manages to get convulsions and turns purple. Mamma gives up on dragging her to the pastry shop. That night she reports the episode to our father. Of my sister she says: "Poor thing, the little creature is so greedy and then those fits of anger, she feels really ill." Of me she says: "Miki told on her sister, she's jealous, for shame!"

(In front of me the icy sea expands, spreading to the horizon with its undulating motion. So white and full of frozen hollows it seems more impassable than in summer when the ships go by, even if they tell me that the Finns came as far as Riga in certain very cold winters, gliding over the sea in their sleds. It's immobile, but I know that it's seething underneath, that it wants to come out like the Düna in spring when it cracks its blanket of ice, and at night I hear it flowing with the sound of thunder.)

Inside me a thought boils up when my mother says, "For shame." It boils up frigid and green: "Me, she would have punished!"

More than a thought—a thought, in fact, is swift and subtle like a cut—it's an immense flood of rage and impotence, a stain with fluctuating edges that seeks to invade me completely. I have to hold it firm inside, but now it's reached the tips of my fingers as they turn down the covers on the bed of my one-eyed doll. One eye fell inside her head, and the doll doctor wasn't able to fix it. I keep her like that and it makes me sick. But I keep her just the same: I won't be like my mother.

An unexpected response while I silently turn down the covers for the one-eyed doll: I won't be like my mother. Unexpected and antithetical to the other, which is also present and conscious: I will be like my mother.

Thoughts that I can almost not think, they're not even in my head, maybe they're huddled in some dirty hole of mine, when suddenly I break something, though I'm trying to be good and smart, better and smarter than my sister, who doesn't give a damn about being good and smart.

No one would pay attention if I said that Mamma prefers Sisi to me. "For shame," they'd say, "Mamma gives you everything she gives your sister."

There's nothing she's had that I've had less of.

When, stock-still behind the living room door, we hear the paper rustling on the packages that Mutti is arranging under the tree and the smell of needles scorched by a candle mixes with the aroma of the brown spice cookies on the oven rack in the kitchen, as many nice, carefully chosen gifts await me as my sister. She has pretty dresses and so do I; until adolescence our clothes are the same.

When I get sick, Mamma takes care of me.

But every so often at the bottom of one of my dirty invisible holes I think—one of those two-faced, conflicting thoughts—that even if I'm a coward and a liar (it's true), my mother shouldn't report it to others. Why does she always tell others everything about these flaws of mine?

I'm three years old—my mother recounts—and I'm always complaining that my stomach hurts. Also, I have no appetite and hand pieces of buttered bread to our dog or ask Mamma to send them to the starving children in Africa. She takes me to the pediatrician, who prescribes Vaseline oil. After a few spoonfuls I'm cured. When my mother asks the doctor if he considers it possible that even though I'm so little I invented everything, he—German and Lutheran— responds that even newborns lie.

I remember quite clearly sitting at the feet of a sofa on which my paternal grandmother is discussing with someone a girl who died of appendicitis. She describes the symptoms, the negligence of the parents, the rapid and inevitable end. I recall touching my stomach because while my grandmother was speaking I felt a little pain.

I don't remember anything else, as I don't recall my particular lies. But I remember very well some stories I told when I was around six or seven. Growing out of the brief, self-justifying lies told by my sister or the maid, mine were beautiful, elaborate lies, in which what was true—and I distinguished it perfectly—was the core around which I arranged the details of the story.

Sometimes there was an element of reality that, inessential at first sight, struck me, and a story would take off from that image. The stories I told myself as well.

For example, the staircase my mother descended dragging my screaming sister by the arm had a wide, open curve, a curve that from then on triggered my fantasies of flight.

I'm a liar and guilty, and my nightmares punish me for my transgressions.

A short, terrible nightmare that stayed with me until I was an adult: the witch dream.

The first time—I think the summer I was seven—I dreamed I was in the street; two bent old ladies pass by in front of me, heads covered by scarves. I'm calm, I'm taking a walk and I'm alone. One of the two old ladies turns and looks at me just as she goes by. She has the terrible face of a witch. I wake up. The nightmare consists only in the instantaneous exposing of that face which I know is "invincible," and against which I can do nothing.

The last time I dreamed the witch dream she herself freed me with her words.

It was a dream of flight: we were fleeing in a group, a group of teenagers—my children didn't appear in the dream, but in fact I was already married and a mother. The dream is suffused with a single violet-black color. The color of a disease, a plague that we are fleeing, and the scrubland we're crossing is the same color. Passing through a village of dirty cottages, I see a large fat woman appear in the doorway of a hut. She has a swollen violet-black face. If she touches me, I'll get sick, too, and die. The woman looks at me and I say: "I'm not afraid of you, I'll go by just the same and I won't get sick." Then she starts laughing, she laughs freely, loud (as if she weren't sick), and says to me: "Of course you can go by, *because you have courage!*"

One day in the house with the big staircase—the last one we lived in in Riga—my father questions me. We're alone in the living room.

He asks me about the preceding summer when we were with Mamma in Torre Pellice; a colleague of my uncle's came to see us every day, a professor with a Spanish surname, who had white teeth and eternally lustrous hair. My father asks me if that man and my mother often talked.

And that man? And Mamma? And here the words begin to come out, all warm, all ready and new. Of course, Mamma and that man often talked in the evening, sitting on the green bench, under the living room window. One night while they were chatting, he gave her something sparkling. A ring? I don't know, I couldn't see clearly, I was in the house. A bracelet? Maybe, but I was in the house and couldn't see clearly.

And on this something sparkling I continue to insist even during the subsequent confrontation with my mother, sitting next to my father on the living room sofa. My mother, unusually gentle: "But really, Miki, tell him it's a lie!" But I, no, I assert that's how it was, just like that.

The truth is that the words would take possession of me: I spoke them and they broke off from my will and pursued their own way, by themselves, intertwining, connecting, forming new shapes. I knew I was giving in to an irrational impulse when I let the words run away from the real point of departure, but I couldn't resist. They overwhelmed me in an irresistible current, they hurled me toward whoever was facing me: I had to try to catch him and drag him with me. I was there in my words, finally emerging from myself, freed from my weak and clumsy gestures. My lie was me, me who could finally strip others of their sentences and their rules, so that they would listen to me just for an instant, and, beyond their adult silences, their deliberate reticence, I would be allowed to take possession of them, to enclose them with me in my circle of light.

The stories I told my sister at night, on the other hand, I constructed out of reality and its details. I never related the fairy tales I read eagerly. In my stories my sister and I were protagonists of adventures and expeditions. There were no fathers and mothers, and adults were often made fun of. We locked the household seamstress in the storeroom. Other times we left for Italy in secret. The adults were stupid and didn't notice what Sisi and I were plotting. I ridiculed them by making them fall down the stairs or walk along the street with wreaths of dried fish around their necks. Talking, I lingered happily on practical details. The places had their names, the days and weeks were specified.

Once, during a walk on the beach—it was fall, we were already wearing quilted jackets—we hid amid the enormous roots of a fir that rose up out of the sand and formed a real den. Our governess, after calling us for a while in a loud voice, left, thinking we had gone ahead on the walk home. After a certain time had elapsed, we followed her on the same road. When we got home, we found that Mamma was not at all alarmed, in fact was almost amused, having assumed the adventure was my sister's idea. That irritated me. I had again missed an opportunity for getting points.

Trapped in my more and more complex, more and more inexplicably useless lies, I continued to follow the damn unstated rules. I was engaged in a constant, if cautious, operation of exposing the lie not only of my neighbor but also of the reality that appeared in unexpected and, it seemed to me, illusory shapes.

It's summer and we're with our governess at a hotel on the shores of a lake. We're playing in the sand in our bathing suits; I'm playing with a small Finn named Arndt. He's in love with me.

I'm always in love. Boys are handsome, unfortunately they're a little stupid. My nursery school classmate who already wears below-the-knee pants, knickerbockers, is handsome. He's old, he should be in school, but he's stupid, so he goes to nursery school.

Once Aunt Jo, my sister's godmother, comes to see us, with her own son, who is very tall, he's ten and is really stupid. He spells out the words letter by letter when he reads, while I who am barely five read fluently. When he's about to leave, I pull my mother aside and beg her: "Ask him to stay for dinner, I like him a lot." My mother smiles but doesn't say anything to him, and they leave. Later she tells about my request, and smiles, surprised and kindly.

I'm not in love with the Finn—he's a year younger than I am (he's six), and I'm a little afraid that the situation would seem preposterous—but I'm happy to play with him: he's very accommodating and he listens to me. When his father comes to see him, he takes us on long boat trips on the lake. He rows for hours in silence and the two of us, in silence, sit in the boat as it glides through the gently rustling reeds.

In some places the lake is covered with water lilies. When you pick them—but it's better not to, because they fade immediately—you hear a distant *plop*, down in the water, and the flower, smelling of dampness, rises obediently into your hand.

Arndt's father doesn't speak, he holds his pipe tight between his teeth and every so often looks at us with his gray eyes. I like going out in the boat with him, especially because he doesn't want anyone else to come on the outing. Only me. I'm sitting behind him and I'm not afraid: if I fell in the lake, he'd pull me out immediately. He's very sad because he's getting divorced, and I think I'd like to marry him. Too bad he's so much older than I am; the hair at his temples is already gray.

So one day, while we're playing in the sand, I see that Arndt has a little sack in his underpants, right in front, between his legs.

"Hey," I say, "why did you put a bag of sand in your underpants?

"It's not a bag of sand," he says, "I've always had it."

"Come on, you've always had it!"

"I have, I've always had it, it's skin, attached in front."

The liar. How is it possible? But he insists.

So I propose that he should prove it that night. While our governesses were chatting as usual in the living room of the rented apartment where he was staying with his, we'd shut ourselves in the bedroom: I would pull down my underpants and he would, too, and so that famous sack of skin would be visible.

At night, with the door closed, we get undressed in the room that's gray in the summer night. I take off my underpants, but he hops up and down and with his hands tightens his around his waist. He even starts shouting when I get insistent.

Our governesses knock at the door and he opens it. I just have time to put on my underpants when they burst in yelling. They dress us and I'm brought back to the hotel. I have to go to bed immediately. With the blanket up to my nose, I hear them talking about "shame." But from time to time they laugh excitedly.

I'm angry. With him, the coward, who didn't keep his side of the bargain. Because he had nothing to show, of course! Then I begin to worry: I'm afraid that the next day the entire hotel will hear this story. And to think that I had gained a good reputation because I sometimes help take orders in the dining room and do the bills. I'm really good at doing the bills.

And now it will all crumble because of the stupid business of taking off our underpants. An unstated rule. When my mother—traveling in Italy at the time—finds out, she, too, will say: "For shame!" Especially when she finds out it wasn't him, it was me who persuaded him to show proof.

The coward, I'll never speak to him again.

In the other room the governesses won't stop chatting and laughing. Every so often they raise their voices and scold the air: "For shame!" But to tell the truth, I'm not at all ashamed; I'm just sorry, and bitterly, for my loss of prestige—that I do regret. But I'm not ashamed.

The fact is, I'm right, too.

It was true that my mother and the Spaniard with the lustrous hair talked softly on the green bench in the garden, even if that talk was only the core of a reality that I hadn't known how to represent except as an imaginary sparkling precious object.

Adults play a dishonest game: let's see what you can guess. We won't say "you're getting warmer" or "colder"; the clues to the right path are hidden here and there in our conversations. It's up to you to pick them up!

But it's a dangerous game; if I get too close, I risk falling into "shame," like the blazing pyre of orange flames I fell into once in a dream trying to escape the usual black locomotive that was pursuing me. When I fell into the fire, fear was mixed with an astonishing pleasure, and the moment I woke the pyre was transformed through successive orange and yellow layers into my parents' bedroom, or rather, into their bed, covered by an orange bedspread.

In that bedroom my mother wore her nightgown and my father pajamas; not even adults could be naked together.

Going around the house in pajamas wasn't allowed either, even though my father did it, naturally. We wore pajamas because we were still children. As adults we would have long hair and would make babies because we were women.

At the beach many people went swimming naked in the freezing-cold water. There was a schedule for it. We went to the beach during the time when you had to swim in a suit and during the time for nude women. My sister, sent one day to see if the nude hour was over, returned saying that she couldn't tell if the people on the beach were men or women, since they were naked.

Once when we were in the park with the governess, I walked off, silently offended by some observation, and went up over the top of the small artificial hill we were on to vent my bad mood. Suddenly some boys emerged from the shrubs scattered in the flower beds beside the downhill path and rushed toward me shouting loudly, "Pee." I turned and began running up the path. I ran very fast with my long legs, and in a moment was at the top, my heart pounding in my chest. I slowed my pace on the way down and didn't tell what had happened.

But why "pee"? The dirty, incongruous word—did they want me to pee on the flower beds?—that the boys had shouted scared me and made me curious. But because in general I lived in a climate of ordeal, I glimpsed a divine judgment—I had been punished for my disobedience—in that event. Those divine judgments that struck every so often distracted and befuddled me, since all things forbidden were shameful and subject to punishment.

We're at the zoo, and in a loud voice I ask the governess what the little red carrot going back and forth on the chimpanzee's lower belly is. I'm scolded for asking in such a loud voice, and the unreasonable violence of the scolding strikes me right away. Yet I don't associate it with the chimpanzee's absurd little carrot, especially since a little while earlier I'd provoked the derision of the onlookers by commenting on some birds of prey with completely mad expressions perched on the branches in the cages. Their necks are bare and bleeding, plucked, as if they'd torn off each other's feathers. And wouldn't they have pecked out our eyes as soon as they could? Look, this girl's scared of everything! But what if a guard inadvertently left a cage open . . . !

I never get it right.

I'm never sure of my gestures: there's no harmony between me and the space around me! When I move, I have to extricate myself from countless invisible knots. Once, our Polish driver—he's Polish, they said at home, but he's nice—teaches me to project shadow figures on a lighted wall, positioning his hands, pulled into fists, in different ways, a rabbit, a dog, a mouse, and even the head and arms of a puppet. The game enchants me so much that every night I practice making the figures; one night, lowering a finger, I see my rabbit lower his ear. For the first time I had managed to change with a gesture something outside of me, even if it was a shadow that couldn't be touched.

I have always loved the free movements of others, and yearned for them.

A young priest walks with long, rapid strides at the head of a funeral procession. His black cassock flaps around his legs, which are hidden but still can be immediately imagined, nimble, impatient, ready for flight.

In the courtyard at school some girls are doing calisthenics; one of them, a passive teenager with a slightly puffy, pale face, who sits in the last row in class, here in the blue uniform, is lithe. She extends one arm and follows the slow, harmonious movement with her gaze. She's absorbed in her arm, she is her arm, entirely.

With the same gaze a boy in a leather jacket is stopped at a street corner, legs astride the saddle of his motorbike, leaning with his head to one side to hear the motor roar. He has a faint, dreamy smile.

I always remain inside myself; all I know is how to walk. From the height of the old mare they've put me on for a ramble in the woods, I look with nostalgia at the yellow grass just cleared of snow, which the wretched beast leans forward to taste, lowering its head, a last bulwark between me and the void. If only I could walk by myself, choosing my own dry path amid the lingering patches of snow!

I learn to blow my nose at around eight. I read *Die Leiden des jungen Werthers* and with the handkerchief I barely wipe off the dripping snot. I wouldn't dream of blowing it out violently, with that horrible sound. And if my brains blew out at the same time, like young Werther's?

I am seldom free of my awkwardness.

Late one afternoon during the summer at the lake, we were surprised by a storm when we were in the middle of the lake on the hotel's big motorboat. We had gone with our father, who had come to visit, to the opposite shore, from which he would leave for Riga. Suddenly, on the way back, the sky turned black, the water rose up in a gigantic crest, and the rain crashed down on us, thundering through continual flashes of lightning.

Someone started shouting, but after a moment of terror, as the storm increased in intensity, with the thunder and lightning amid gusts of wind, and I was streaming with water, I felt touched by an irresistible force that cancelled out my fear. I don't remember who was with me—certainly my sister and the governess—I remember the lake and the rain. When we reached the shore, I ran to the hotel and, forgetting the clumsiness of my gestures, took off my shoes in the lobby.

Otherwise I was oppressed by "good manners."

From a curtsey on the street to elbows drawn in alongside at the table. I couldn't escape "good manners."

Once Sisi and I climb up on the windowsill of the game room and expose our bottoms to the really rude children of the Swedish ambassador opposite us. The women selling fish at the market usually did that to customers who didn't appreciate their fish. "It's not fresh? See if this seems fresher!"

Someone comes from there to inform on us, and we're scolded. We hadn't displayed "good manners." And to think that those loutish Swedes, full of themselves like all Swedes, were constantly provoking us.

Who didn't have "good manners"?

Well, besides the fishmongers, the mailman, and the butcher, also the Russian coachmen who blew their noses with their fingers and the peasants of the Polish corridor you saw from the windows of the train in their filthy hovels. And the Russian priests who come out in solemn procession from their big church with the grand gilded cupolas, wearing purple vestments and gold embroidery, but who—"What a stink!"—never wash.

I'm really interested in people who don't have good manners. I don't dare speak to them, but I try to understand how in the world they manage not to respect the rules. It seems to me that they live very well without rules. I don't envy them, though: they're poor and it's terrible to be poor.

The cook and the maid talk about the existence of God. The cook says that God is "only" pure spirit and isn't interested in our doings. I'm gripped by panic, but naturally I can't express it in questions or words.

I wouldn't know now if that distress was due to the term "spirit," which at first seemed to me to evoke a ghost, or if it was instead the tiny *nur* (only) that chilled me: it put God at a distance with an unaffected serenity, the same with which the cook confidently took her famous strudel out of the oven. The same serenity as the driver's when he tells me how, swerving too quickly on a stretch of gravel, he hurled a cousin of my father's out of the car. Or how he arrived at the central station in Riga driving, again in our car, on the tracks. He was drunk—the Poles are often drunk—and he even admitted it. He laughed, saying that he was drunk and that my father had had to pay a big fine for the business of the central station; he also laughed when he repeated in his rather poor German—but he didn't care about that—that the cousin had broken "only" a leg and an arm.

One Saturday afternoon we go with our governess to help her mother, who had moved. We had to paste a pink-flowered wallpaper on the walls of a room that I found quite small. The mother of our governess was small, too, and fat and chatty. She was suspected of remote southern origins. Polish, in other words.

There was warm paste in a basin. The small old woman chatted and laughed the whole time. She was happy with her flowered wallpaper.

I was pleased: I helped stretch out the wallpaper and I liked seeing the wall get covered with flowers and become clean and happy. I would have liked to go every Saturday to paste wallpaper. I would have liked to have a small room all for myself, in which there was also, as here, a stove to cook on. Everything gathered around me, carefully put away, as I had put away in a metal box that could be closed with a hook the few things I wanted to take with me when I fled to Italy.

We were Latvian because we were born in Riga. Even my mother, who was Italian, had a Latvian passport because she had married my father.

We are registered on our mother's Latvian passport, and in school in the Latvian class we learn the hymn *God Save Latvia*.

For one night in November every year, a row of little lights are placed between the double panes of the windows: it's Latvia's independence celebration. The lights shine, spreading in the windows of the whole city. My father grumbles that Kārlis Ulmanis—the prime minister of Latvia—is a pig. My father doesn't like premiers. In the meantime I've learned that Mussolini isn't a runner but the prime minister of Italy. Mamma teaches us a song—whose words we don't understand—that begins: *Giovinezza, giovinezza* . . . I like singing it because it's an Italian song.

The Latvian anthem is slow and solemn and difficult to sing by yourself. I like singing by myself, even if I can't carry a tune like my sister. I sing when I'm playing and I sing when I'm walking in the park during our outings, if I'm sure no one can hear me. Singing on the street is extremely rude.

Every morning at school, lined up by class in the big hall where at Christmas the sacred pageant of the birth of Christ was performed—I was always in the audience and never had the privilege even of being an angel, broad wings sprinkled with silver powder—we sang a chorale in chorus, after the prayer.

I sang those chorales again in Torre Pellice—many were by Luther—following the stanzas in the book of texts I'd saved. Today I sing some of them at Christmas, when I'm alone in the house.

Singing aloud together. If you're not in tune the person next to you covers you with the correct note. Singing in a chorus, lined up, all in harmony.

In class we usually sang old German songs: a young man is about to die in the red dawn, and another, young and bold, also dies, after "disloyally" abandoning father and mother.

"Oh Strassburg, oh Strassburg"! Why do we die for you? And why then "disloyally"? And why doesn't the soldier run away but stops to sing, asking his brave comrade if the bullet is coming toward him or toward the other?

And yet even "not understanding" can be very satisfying if it's accompanied by music. For example, the text of the chorale "A *rosellino*—a rose—has sprung up from a tender root . . ." is really incomprehensible given what follows—among other things, who is Jesse?—not to mention that it should be *una rosellina*. Anyway it doesn't matter; it's lovely to sing, with the meaningless words reeling out one from the other, rising and then falling in cascades.

Whereas the piano chords that breathlessly race after the father galloping with the sick child are grim and repeated. The elf king is hidden in the dark rustling around them. Might he be the alder king? Actually he has a name with a mysterious sound, halfway between elf and alder: *Erlkönig*. I've never seen an elf and maybe not an alder, but that sound with the hard *r* in the middle of the word evokes a spiteful "almost elf" that hidden among the leaves causes sick babies to die. The Erlkönig's presence came from the piano chords and slowly pervaded the room, much more real than Prime Minister Ulmanis.

And so, singing, I developed a nostalgia for escape that drew me away without a country (or rules) toward no goal, from under the linden tree into whose bark I'd carved names dear and unnamed.

The unnamed names—like the sound of the piano and the held breath of the winter wind when it's about to hurl itself, whirling, across the snowy plain—attract me, submerge me in a secret expectation, more than the named names, which you always have to think about precisely.

In fact there are many named names, and you have to know them all and keep them in order and never lose them. Like your passport. If you lose your passport, you go to prison.

I'm Latvian and Christian, so they told me. I believe it, even though I have to hold these names tight in the palm of my hand like hard objects. It's a burden that I have to carry along with the other rules. I'm Latvian, but I speak German and I don't understand who Jesus Christ is. How he ended up on the cross right out of the nativity crèche, having grown up, like me, in a single night. As a child he has a mother, Mary, as an adult a father—not unnamed though better not to name—but who crucified him? Probably the other unnamable, "the spiteful enemy of man in ancient times."

One morning we enter the cathedral, where the darkness extends high over our heads. From the pulpit the priest speaks in a loud voice and pointing his finger scolds an old man in the middle of the crowd, right next to me, leaning on a stick and trembling. I'm torn between the fear of being confused with the old man—might the priest think we're together?—and an immense pity for him. I don't understand why the priest is mad at him, so old and trembling, and I want to leave.

At night, the other unnamable "enemy of man" is hidden under my bed. I don't believe he's black and horned, as in the story of the "devil's grandmother" that I saw performed in a show for the schools. I've also seen "Max and Moritz" come out flat, entirely flat, in the form of cookies on the rack of a huge oven, condemned to that fate by their repeated acts of disobedience. Everybody laughs, I don't laugh: their squashed human form makes me shudder. I don't even laugh when I see the devil's grandmother pull a hair out of his beard while he sleeps. He isn't like that. He doesn't have horns and a tail but is much more frightening, coagulated into an irrational corporeality, like elves and fairies. He doesn't come to punish me—for that, adults and my nightmares are sufficient—he comes because he has to find a place to exist. I can't recall how long he's been under my bed, maybe forever.

God won't help me get rid of him; I have to do it by myself. God is in Heaven and only sometimes smiles at me in a childish song that goes: "Look how many clouds pass by in the big vault of the sky; look how many stars are in the big, big world. God, the Lord, has counted them, may he not miss even one." In bed, pinching the hem of my pajama sleeve between two fingers, I repeat the song, and, thanks to God's counting what is impossible to count—this I know—it submerges me like a certainty and I fall asleep. At the same time he falls asleep under my bed.

My Latvian grandfather and my Russian grandmother are Jewish. My Italian grandparents—who in fact are also part French—are Waldensian[3]. My mother is Waldensian. Some Latvians—the most stupid—are Catholics. But Aunt Jo is Catholic, and she isn't in the least stupid. Petkevic, our driver, is also Catholic. The Poles are Catholics. The Russians

---

3 The Waldensians were a Christian movement that arose in France in the twelfth century, joined the Reformation in the sixteenth, and over the centuries were persecuted, suppressed, and often forced into exile. They are now concentrated mainly in the Alpine valleys of Piedmont west of Turin.

are Orthodox, but my Russian grandmother is Jewish. On the other hand the Russians at the Soviet Embassy aren't Orthodox. They're like my father: they have no religion. They're very mean and won't let anyone pass on the sidewalk in front of their door. They could shoot you! They called Petersburg Leningrad and shot the tsar and his family. But the tsar was far from a saint and he in turn shot people who didn't shout "Long live the tsar." He was Orthodox; among all religions, the Orthodox is hardly a religion.

No one explains to me the difference between Jews and Christians. Again they're names that I have to accept as they are. My father was brought up by a Lutheran pastor—as a child he was extremely lively, a rebel, said Grandfather, and Grandmother didn't feel up to raising him, and so they sent him away, something he never forgave his parents for, said my mother—and he was as attached to that pastor as he could be, said my mother. Nevertheless he had made trouble for Mamma when she decided to send us to the German Lutheran school. He had said: "They're Jewish, why are you sending them to the Lutheran school?"

He said it to annoy Mamma: we weren't Jews, we had been baptized—I in Torre Pellice, at a year old (my father was in fact present at the ceremony), and my sister at four, in her pink silk dress, during a vacation at the Strand[4]. She had shaken the drops of water off her skirt with an impatient hand.

---

4 The Strand, or Riga Strand, was a beach resort on the Baltic about fifteen miles west of Riga.

When you're baptized you're no longer a Jew: probably it's a step forward.

I love my Latvian grandfather, Mosè, whom at home they called Moritz. Now when I talk about him I say "my little grandfather." Mamma objected, saying that Grandfather wasn't at all little; maybe he seemed small compared with my father.

Grandfather had very black eyes under bushy white eyebrows. Sometimes on Saturday afternoons we went to our grandparents' house; we played in Grandfather's study, under his desk. At night, when we stayed for dinner, there was an egg in the shell and Grandpa cut off the tip with a single swipe.

Grandfather told us the story of when he was young and wanted to marry Grandmother. He was very poor, she was rich and had studied at a boarding school for "aristocratic" girls in Vitebsk. In order to marry her Grandfather had gone to Siberia to become a fur trader; when he got rich, he had bought the tannery and married Grandmother.

One day Grandfather brings us a bag of many different-colored banknotes. "Play," he tells us. And then he says that he keeps those beautiful bills in bags in the attic. It's his savings in the tsar's rubles, now worthless.

With Grandfather I play at counting; it amuses him to see me do sums so fast.

In school I'm by far the best in mathematics. When I raise my hand to answer, forty large, tall, blond German girls, my classmates, are sitting around me in silence. That repays me, at least a little, for my embarrassing failures on the Swedish ladder, where I stay stuck between the lower bars, surrounded by the same large, blond, stolid silence. It repays me only in a minimal way, because unfortunately being good at school is a duty. Mamma and my sister aren't good at math, but being good at math doesn't win you any points.

Whereas numbers send me into raptures—which is considered a little *unheimlich* (creepy)—and when I'm not reading or playing, I make increasingly long, increasingly difficult calculations. I'm not interested in the measurements of my room, but I make calculations that go beyond the stars, far beyond, maybe approaching close to him whom it's more prudent not to name. My numbers are a ladder that ascends and has no end.

When I lose myself like that among the zeroes, I regret that it's a duty to be good at school, that you get no credit for being able to rapidly multiply 2340 by 2500; on the other hand Mamma was also really good at school—if not in math, in all the rest—and her father, my Waldensian grandfather, who had a narrow, sculpted face with a straight nose and thin lips, harassed her about her grades because he was a teacher in the school she went to, the Collegio di Torre Pellice. When she'd go hiking in the mountains on Sunday, on Monday morning he interrogated her right away and was even stricter with her than with the others, who called him "the scourge."

Mamma decided that she would never torment her daughters about grades. Never praise, either, of course. And she impartially applied the first rule to my sister, the second to me.

My grandfather Mosè praised me and I loved him, cautiously and without saying so, because Mamma didn't love him at all, and that put a curtain between him and me, a curtain of questioning and checking on his actual feelings toward Mamma. I didn't think he disliked her, as she said. Hadn't I seen him one day stop our father in the doorway—we were all at our grandparents'—to keep him from running after Mamma, who had said something to him, then had rapidly run out of the house? Grandfather had put himself between him and the door and closed it behind Mamma. Then he had scolded our father in a loud, harsh voice. He wasn't afraid of him.

Later, in Torre Pellice, my mother told me that Grandfather had testified against her in the divorce case because she was a Christian and "Jews are always in agreement against Christians." That deeply distressed and grieved me: my memory of Grandfather—who died of an illness a few months after Grandmother, in 1940—emerged from it diminished, different from the way I held him in my secret affections. I knew that he was "just" in his heart and I wondered why he had been unfaithful to me.

Forty years later, reading for the first time my parents' final divorce decree—a document that had been kept among my mother's papers, which I was reorganizing—I found some information that consoled me: my grandparents, witnesses at the trial, had both stated that they considered it better for us to be handed over to our mother rather than to their son. So he was restored to me, although in the guise of the witness Mosè Gersoni, my dear grandfather.

When we sang our Lutheran hymns, he listened attentively. Once, suddenly raising his voice, he sided with me against my sister. I had sung that God was the one who helps, and Sisi that he was the one who saves; so Grandfather—brusque, raising his voice—had observed that God helps and doesn't save.

Grandfather is the only adult who speaks to me about God.

Mamma forgot to prepare me for the religion exam for admission to the Lutheran school. I was eight. I was asked, "Who is God?" and, gripped by panic, I didn't know how to answer. How could I not compromise myself?

God is just, Grandfather says, but we can't understand his justice. I don't like that, I ponder it, it's sort of like the story of how the mother loves her children because she suffered bringing them into the world. It's not at all rational.

But faith isn't rational, they explain at school. So I do my own private test. On the way home one morning, I pick up a dead mouse in the snow. I keep it in the dresser drawer of my dollhouse. Every night I pray to make it come back to life. But it doesn't come back to life, and when it turns soft I have to throw it away. And similarly, the opposite—despite my prayers, the stepmother of a classmate to whom I'd promised a miracle doesn't die. (When you pray, you can safely name God.)

I don't tell anyone about these experiments of mine; only my sister knows, she's cynical but loyal. She informs me right away that the mouse won't come back to life and the stepmother won't die, but she keeps the secret.

I don't tell Grandfather: Grandfather doesn't believe that a person can come back to life; I'm really sorry about it for him because he's old and sick. Less for Grandmother, since no particular feeling binds me to her. I hardly ever see her, because she's often out walking with Aunt Betty, our father's sister; when she's home, Grandfather says to her in a tender and worried tone: "Aren't you tired, Anna, don't you want to rest for a while?" Sometimes she gets out of bed and plays waltzes on the piano for us: Sisi and I dance around the room.

One afternoon Grandmother invites some heavily made-up and jeweled ladies for tea. Among them, I'm told, is our father's first wife; when I pass by the table, she observes me attentively. I think it's because of my hair; I've inherited from Grandmother Anna its dark blond color. Everyone else in the family has black hair.

Grandmother often repeats: my emeralds are for the little girls. I don't remember having ever seen them, but I'm glad to inherit them along with the hair, even though according to the rules wearing too much jewelry is in bad taste. It's also in bad taste for children to wear furs. Not even Jewish children had fur coats. And it was in bad taste to drive children to school; they had to learn to walk there by themselves.

My father's relatives were in general people with bad taste. Uncle Talrose—Aunt Betty's husband, whom Grandfather couldn't bear—was a millionaire, and miserly. I knew that from their Christian maid Marta, whom they lent some days to my grandparents.

In their dark, dusty house, the maid Marta lived in a tiny room near the green-colored kitchen. Once I heard Grandfather observe about some misdeed of Marta's that the poor girl was Christian and therefore crazy. Grandfather had used the Yiddish words *goy* and *meschugge* instead of the German that he usually spoke, probably so that I wouldn't understand; but I understood perfectly well, and so I felt it my duty to demonstrate to Marta my Christian solidarity. I went to the kitchen and tried to converse with her in that greenish air. She kept repeating that the Jews are miserly and my aunt and uncle wouldn't take care of her teeth. She said she wanted to return to the country and, patting her stomach, groaned in an unseemly way. She was a very unlikable Christian and certainly a bit *meschugge*. I went back to the dining room.

One day we went with our father to a party with his relatives. There was a very long table—maybe twenty people—it was either Passover or the wedding of my cousin Benno. All my father's relatives with bad taste talked at the same time in loud voices. Someone sang. I was sitting with my elbows drawn in along my sides, and in that very small space I was left perfectly in peace; it was as if that place were mine anyway. I could have shifted my elbows and no one would have said anything.

There was stained glass in the windows. Was that good taste or bad?

I didn't know any of my father's relatives. I seldom saw them and, since I wasn't at all interested in people's doings—and didn't much understand them—I never remembered whom they were married to or divorced from, whose children were whose, and barely what their jobs were. I remember distinctly only Aunt Betty, good-natured and jovial, and my two cousins Benno and Saul, who were much older than we were. Benno—he was kind and affectionate—for fun once stuck me in one of his boots; he was doing his military service. Saul offered me my first Turinese pastries in his room, I think in Via Garibaldi. He was studying medicine in Turin and would practice his profession in Latvia. I found the pastries ridiculously small, but much more suited to me than the gigantic pastries of Riga.

My cousins, my aunts and uncles, the others at the table didn't survive 1941.

After my father and mother separated, I never saw my grandparents again, or any of our father's family. Of that day of celebration I remember the strange impression made by hearing someone say of us: "Here are Sammy's kids." I wasn't used to being attributed to our father, or at least to our father without our mother's name being added.

In fact I wasn't used to the idea of belonging to a family. I didn't say "my parents," but *Vati* and *Mutt*, and after their separation "my father" and "my mother." Still remote from my feelings and my reflections was the meaning of the court's assertion, while it gave custody to our mother, that both had treated us well, each contributing for his or her part to our well-being.

My only childhood bond was with my sister. Constant and unexamined. My family was her and me: I never wondered what she thought of me and even my jealousy toward her didn't erode my attachment. That had to do with my mother. In the circle of light my sister was always with me, but I didn't have to make any special mention of it.

She recalls different details of many of the episodes I've recounted, and of some, despite the common experience I've described, she has a completely opposite view.

Regarding the episode of the stairs she recalls that she ate the top layer of a box of candied pineapple—so she was licking off sugar, not cream—and she recalls that on the top of the box was written "Göttingen." And she claims that on the stairs she was yelling not with rage but with terror because Mamma was threatening her with life in prison. When we were in the castle at the edge of the forest, she rescued and brought inside no fewer than twenty-one birds of passage found stiff with cold and about to die on the road. Without the help of any prayer they thawed in the warmth and started flying away through the doors. She says also that she learned to swim with the other kids on the farm while I was in bed with scarlet fever. They swam in the clear, clean river that ran downhill from the farm and I, in bed, reread *The Jungle Book* for the fourth time. She maintained a certain Latvian patriotism and insists that I wouldn't speak to the mailman because I was a snob. It seems, also, that I liked to go to parties, at one of which we were given little rings. I remember a certain disappointment because the stone was ruby red and not blue; the ring had been put on the handle of the spoon that went with the little cups on a long table.

As for our father, Sisi says that in the months when Mamma lived somewhere else he would take her out at night while I was already sleeping my Lutheran sleeps. So Sisi sat at Otto Schwarz, one of the famous pastry shops of Riga, and ate all the pastries she wanted; our father, meanwhile, played poker with his friends until two in the morning.

Talking over our childhood, I discovered that, in an unusual and nonliterary coincidence, we both remembered as the most beautiful moments our strolls along the seashore in summer sunsets, when we walked barefoot for miles, looking for bits of amber that could be found mixed in with the black debris of seaweed and driftwood deposited along the line of the waves: we went out in the extended, luminous evening that would never become night and the sand had the same silver-white color as the sky; it seemed that we would never have to turn back but would continue barefoot along the sea in whose calm you couldn't distinguish even the lapping of the water when it reached the beach. Every so often we'd bend down to pick up a transparent orange fragment that we put in a matchbox.

We left Latvia one morning in July of 1935. Our departure had been delayed by an illness of mine, the usual stupid inconvenient childhood illness. I had caught scarlet fever after trying to hatch a goose egg for several days, in a bush behind the farm. I had attributed the chills of the fever to the usual divine punishment for an attempt I felt was vaguely sacrilegious. Mamma had taken care of me for the long weeks of bed rest that scarlet fever then required, and I had learned to read French from the magazines she was reading.

We had to leave from an outlying station because our father had private police watching the central station in Riga. We were loaded onto a farm cart with our baggage and we set out through the woods, the same where, a few nights earlier, on the eve of the feast of San Giovanni, from the window of my room I had seen the peasants' torches disappear.

When we entered the wandering shadows of the forest, I saw next to the cart the goslings born two weeks earlier. They walked a few steps with us, then stopped. I began to cry, a long desperate cry. I was leaving them in their soft yellow feathers and wouldn't see them grow up and swim later in the stream.

Behind me, as in a game whose moves were now fixed forever, my childhood stopped with them, on the luminous edge of the woods.

Pity and Anger

For Cecilia,
who knows true pity

In recent years, as the astonishment of discovering that I, too, am getting older sweeps over me, I continue to dream—almost in compensation—beautiful, bright-colored, uninterrupted dreams, as if instead of dreaming I were writing, and on one of those rare occasions when a page pleases me immediately. Then I wake up satisfied, or maybe rather than satisfied—the word could suggest a contentedness I don't feel—I wake up soothed, since even awake I recall those dreams roaming freely inside me much more precisely than many real events; they have the mark of something completed, even, let's say, irrevocable, stated not with regret but instead as one might say, That's how it is, it can't be otherwise, the circle is closed and within that circle your life stands still in all its colors, but not one more.

I dreamed, for example, of walking along the streets of an entirely Gothic city together with nameless friends; the architraves of the portals were carved as if they had been wood, and so, too, were the cornices of the windows and even the edges of the sidewalks. Of the colors of the sculptures I recall mainly a carmine red that in the dream I liked immensely.

Another time, I entered a courtyard I had glimpsed in

reality during a period when I was wandering through Turin neighborhoods in search of a courtyard suitable for a film to be based on a book of mine. The courtyard was bursting with white flowers, their petals transparent but the clusters full and thick, and someone told me I could pick them; while I gathered a large bunch I heard the sound of cars passing on the other side of the decrepit walls that made up three sides of the courtyard (on the fourth there was a palm tree), and I also heard many people talking inside the run-down buildings. Both the sound of the cars—maybe behind the palm tree there was a highway—and the voices were cheerful. Besides—this was the predominant sensation of the dream— the flowers were wild, and I could pick lots of them, as many as I wanted, and then leave the courtyard freely.

Thus I dreamed many times of returning to Torre Pellice, to the house of my Waldensian grandparents, where I lived between the ages of ten and twenty, placed in the care of my maternal grandmother, after my parents' divorce. The dream leads me continuously from the house to the lawn and from the lawn to the house. This is always open, flooded with sun, and both the ground-floor dining room and the room upstairs where my mother stayed during her sojourns with us are empty of furniture. I am me now and me then; sometimes I know that I have a child or all my children or even my grand-son with me, but I don't see them in the dream. I go from the house to the lawn through the garden, but I don't even see it.

Something always happens on the lawn: once it's full of water, another time it's covered on one side by a long green plastic shed roof that runs above the vines planted by my grandfather, from the boundary wall at the far end up to the chicken coop. Sometimes I realize that the fruit trees have been uprooted, but I don't mind because I know it's part of some work being done on the lawn. There's never anything below the low wall on the right, where a path descended directly through the fields to the Pellice river, and never anything beyond the boundary wall, either.

Sometimes, returning from the lawn to the house, I find myself in the kitchen, which unlike the other rooms is darkened by closed shutters and is full of furniture, pots and pans, dishes, placed all around on tables and shelves. Here and there I also see different foods, which I eat, and they're good, though I don't know what they are.

So I go back and forth and chat with Grandmother—even when I know it's my mother, she has Grandmother's face and words—and talk about my departure for Turin. Grandmother tells me to stay a few days more, the weather is good, I haven't seen any of my old friends. She mentions a friend and neighbor I haven't seen for twenty years. The names of schoolmates come to mind whom I didn't much care about then and haven't thought of since. But yes, I say to myself, I'll stay longer. And here I feel an extraordinary sense of security: yes, I'll stay home, in my home. And I'll eat the good, formless, tasteless food: the sun comes in through the door and the open windows; it's a September sun, warm and the color of gold. I'll go out to the lawn and then return to the house.

Here, constructed by my dream, is a past that didn't exist

and an encounter—with my grandmother and my mother—that didn't exist, either. Words not spoken, or, rather, not spoken in that serene gilded light, in a house that's open, and a little untidy. Once I even dreamed of long, frayed curtains on the dining room windows, which were much bigger than the real ones, curtains of a striped fabric like a beach umbrella, still pierced by the sun's rays.

These bright-colored dreams escorting me from middle age to old age have, it seems to me, a common meaning, even if the images that compose them come from different settings. Whatever their psychological and imaginative material, however—honed as I am by rivers of reflections and recognitions, I could reconstruct it almost piece by piece—they all pretend that I have resolved and accepted. That I no longer fear any encounter. That I am able to look toward the end as it approaches, enjoying all the colors of life.

Or they are a warning of something that might happen but might already have happened—an angelic message that has chosen the pathway of dreams to reach me, since dreams don't have space or time, and surely it's in a dream that the Archangel Gabriel stands firm with his index finger raised. What he indicates with his raised finger will not necessarily happen, or at least it won't necessarily happen in the life of the one who receives the message.

These dreams of mine are, in fact, exempt from the repetitiousness of destiny, a kind of invitation to forget the colorless monotony of events, to erase their outlines, to remove them from time, seizing only the imperceptible change, stationary like the vibration of a dragonfly's wings on the iridescent reflection of the water.

Time entered my life when I arrived in Torre Pellice with my sister. It gave me for the first time a past, a thickness in which to be submerged, avoiding investigations and assaults; the story of my childhood was what remained to me of my preceding existence, since in the space of a few weeks I changed country, language, and family circle.

The alternation of the seasons seemed to mark home life according to ancient peasant customs, though these were far removed from my grandmother, the daughter of a by now well-off bourgeois family.

But year after year the herbs that her mother, a Huguenot from Provence, had brought from her garden near Nîmes to her husband's Waldensian garden continued to reseed in my grandmother's garden, handed down when she married, just as the fine pieces of simple, pale walnut Provençal furniture were handed down from one house to the other.

Wood sorrel, mixed with spinach.

Borage for frittatas and *frittelle*.

Chervil, used not only in frittatas but to season vegetable soups, too. Grandmother also put a pinch of wood sorrel in the frittatas.

Onion grass.

Wild thyme.

Savory, used exclusively, along with parsley, to season peas, during the short season when we ate them, that is, when they were growing in our garden.

All these herbs had French names and so did rhubarb, which Grandmother used in one of her *tartes aux fruits*, and *cren*, horseradish, which was grated to make a seasoning for *bollito*, boiled meat; and there were French names for the kitchen utensils, the furniture, clothes, the fruit in the orchard, the grapes that lay drying on tables in the attic, the slightly bitter chestnut honey.

Also French was the small New Testament, with a shiny black cover and very thin pages, which they bought me as soon as I arrived in Torre Pellice. I liked the little book: you had to turn the pages carefully so as not to tear them, and, since I loved books as physical objects, I still remember the smell. With this New Testament, we went to Sunday school, and the first nonhousehold French I spoke was the verses I had to learn by heart from one Sunday to the next.

All around the house are mountains. Grandmother tells me that when I was a year old and on summer evenings didn't want to sleep, they'd carry me in their arms to the balcony to look at them. And I, who had come from an immense plain, pointed my finger in amazement.

In the background, to the right of the valley, was Monte Granero; in the middle Monte Palavas; in the distance on the left Monte Boucie; just opposite our house, beyond the fields and the Pellice, the hill that rises to Rorà. Then, behind the house—you had to move all the way to the end of the balcony to see it—Monte Vandalino, with Castelluzzo. The mountains don't enclose the valley: on every hill and along the rocky riverbeds are paths, and passes open up through which one can flee to other mountains.

Places were often mentioned in the family, and they, too, carried time within themselves. Butter wrapped in big green leaves and Seirass cheese in fresh hay, as if in a wig, were brought to us from Sella Veja down through Val d'Angrogna, which Grandfather as a child had traversed every day—five kilometers there and five back—to go to school. Sometimes on Sunday we'd walk to the ruins of the fort built by Vittorio Amedeo II. Below it was the old Catholic neighborhood. The Catholics, too, were place and time, undifferentiated, without interruption. They were a wall that was almost never mentioned but that remained present.

The Collegio Valdese, where my sister and I go, isn't far from our house. I carry a notebook on whose inside cover I've pasted a picture of my mother—her pale face is severe over the tailored jacket, which has the small fascist emblem attached to the buttonhole—and I look at it secretly during class. I'm still the smartest in math, and after a few months I discover that my compositions are the best, too.

Doing math homework brings me confidence and peace. I do it with a classmate in a very old house on the edge of town, in the direction of Villar. On one side the slope that descended to the cemetery was covered with vegetable gardens, on the other rose the ancient curving road to Bouissa. We sat in the small kitchen warmed by the stove, on the table an oilcloth and, in order, the paper, the sharpened pencils, the clean eraser. That warm afternoon filled with figures and drawings was swathed in serenity.

But outside I have to adjust continually: something has broken in my sense of time and from now on time will follow an irregular path; like an old clock, it sometimes runs fast, sometimes it will start up again only with a jolt.

I have to restrain the leg that is about to bend in a curt-sey—the metamorphosis had surprised me as I went from the curtsey of a small child to that of a young girl—and loosen my tongue, first in French, then in Italian; I have to get used to the mistaken pronunciation of my last name, fighting for months to correct it to "Ghersoni," then resigning myself.

One morning I'm sitting in what was at the time the Collegio's gym but which also housed the school's theater. I'm listening to the Monday sermon; usually we'd go to a class-room, but perhaps that day was a special occasion. Sitting on the bench I was listening to the minister with my usual attention when suddenly the millenniums spilled out on me and for a second I saw behind him all the peoples on earth in their houses and huts, on the deserts and seas—forever and ever amen—and also on the mountain peaks from which we Waldensians "had been drawn" and I thought: "How is it possible that among all the peoples on earth God favored the Christians?" And answered myself immediately, with an inescapable rational illumination: "It's not possible."

If I put the noun "illumination" next to the adjec-tive "rational" I do so to reduce its size. Those moments which, repeated on other occasions, settled in me forever, those pinpricks, circumscribed in their dimensions but profound, were not miraculous suggestions, they didn't follow the hint of the raised index finger that I like to imagine in my dreams; rather, they expressed in a few codified words, like a conversation in front of a market stall, reflections and emotions—reflections on emotions—of far in the past. And also of far into the future, because although they stayed solidly inside me, like tiny pinpoint glimmers, I continued to ponder, dissolve, and transform the same emotions, the same thoughts that had inspired those moments; even the circumstances that provoked them might have been realized sooner or later and only in that sense can they be seen as illuminations.

I had begun to study history in middle school; I had an excellent memory, and, although I was still very shy, I relaxed when I was explaining the connections between events, between causes and effects and the harmonious interpenetration of time and space. I was fascinated and reassured by history's limitations, by the fact that it had already happened, the words had already been said—and so by the possibility of knowing everything.

I had always liked historical tales. At first the characters seemed to me wrapped in a thick spiderweb of acts and motivations that I was not yet able to understand completely. Bare, with few features, without clothes or costumes—the centuries hadn't yet invaded me—they were often reduced to a single detail that had struck me or even just a feeling they had awakened in me.

At Waltershof I had read two books: one was the story of the last days and execution of Marie Antoinette, the other recounted the adventures of the Germanic tribal leader Arminius. In the Marie Antoinette story I was immediately gripped by the vision of the "bloody head that the executioner picked up and presented to the people." All the rest—including the unfortunate queen's body in costume and without, the clamoring crowd, and even the executioner—paled next to the horrible head; I could identify only with that, if I can put it that way. As I read, a long shudder encircled my neck like a scar. I also have a clear memory of the story's fervent, frenzied tone, and, since I had been taught to consider all exaggerations "insincere," I suspected that I wasn't being told everything. I had been brought up on the "reasonableness," even if cruel, of punishments.

On the other hand the adventures of Arminius (and his men) swept me away. I read the book all in one sitting, and when I reached the end and looked up, the forest beyond the fields was on fire in the sunset, burning Arminius (and his men), who were tied to the trees. At the same time, the book burned, too, with all its adventures: I remember none of them: what stayed with me was stronger and brighter than the tribulations of Arminius, and it was hatred of the *Römer* and their wicked deeds.

When I left Waltershof I left Arminius (and his men) there forever: Arminius with his German name, in his German forest whose trees and flowers I long thought of by their German names (and they were trees and flowers different from the Italian ones). Nor did it occur to me to find out who those hateful *Römer* were. I didn't connect them at all with the Romans in the wretched schoolbooks of fascist Italy; the contrast was too strong and the forest of Teutoburg too far. Only much later, when I read, in German, Theodor Mommsen's *History of Rome*, did I suddenly realize that without noticing I had gone over to the other side.

But studying causes and effects and events—after the millenniums spilled out on me, that morning in the gym, and the centuries began to besiege me, the way the high tide eats away at the beach little by little—I felt fear rising in the face of History. It didn't provide security; on the contrary, it didn't stand still, in a past with impenetrable walls, but filled the world with waves of the dead and then of the living and then of the dead again, operating blind as a seed.

I looked out the classroom windows at the hill of Rorà opposite, white with snow and striped by black rows of trees.

A little farther away on the same hill was the house of Giosué Janavel, the seventeenth-century Waldensian resistance leader, which you could still visit. When the cold disappeared from the mountains, the Catholics of Luserna, chatelaines and soldiers, would go looking for him on the paths that ran in furrows now obscured by earth and stones. And he, with his men or alone, with the help of a boy, would shoot at them with the culverin, the musket he himself had perfected. To keep the faith and fight the good fight. Blessed are those who hunger and thirst after justice for they will be sated.

Meanwhile in class we read the Bible, from Genesis in the first year of middle school to the Apocalypse in the last year of high school—the pages rustled rapidly when the teacher told us to skip certain chapters and, scenting racy passages, we immediately rushed to read them.

Thus Lot lay with his daughters and Solomon compared the breasts of his beloved to two hills crowded with sheep. The discordant animal comparison repulsed me; I found those breasts grazing in the middle of Holy Scripture indecent, nothing to do with the timid itch of my own nipples growing under the black smock.

Besides, I read the Bible on my own as well, I read and reread where it's written that the God who approaches isn't the great wind, isn't the fire, but is, in the end, a sweet subdued music. Or about Moses and the burning bush that's on fire but is not consumed. And then where it's written (the two words next to each other, "it's written," give me peace) "the spirit blows where it will." Yet the Bible often disturbs me; its stories aren't rational, or harmonious, and the causes and effects are obscure, but since I read the Bible the way I read Victor Hugo, Joshua stopping the moon and Jesus walking on water appeared to me as images, not reflections. Because another story was taking place on unknowable pathways behind those images, I was forced to reread. But even then matters of doctrine and theology made me impatient, and I was excited only by a text where the one point I really cared about—which concerned my relations with God—was manifested in a poetic and dramatic form. The whole New

Testament seemed to resound with the final terrible cry of Jesus on the cross: "My God, my God, why have you forsaken me?" If God hadn't taken pity on him, why should he take pity on me?

He was a tremendous God, no longer hidden and counting the stars behind the clouds sketched in my seventeenth-century Lutheran religion book but there, right there, above the Granero, Boucie, Roux, and Guinivert mountains, and hadn't he often descended in the fog to hide an ancestor positioned, with his harquebus, behind a rock or a wall, lying in wait for a Frenchman or a Piedmontese—a papist, in other words? Sometimes he hadn't come down; but the decision was His. You can't make deals with Him, the God of the *barbetti*,[5] the God of my mother's Waldensian forebears.

You can't offer him works, since, if you look carefully, some personal advantage will always be found in the end, something to take to the market, butter or Seirass or veal. Refuse works, but you have to work well, remove the rocks from the fields, carry manure to the pastures in the pannier, help the widow and the old man and listen on Sunday to the pastor's sermon. Not only to learn but to criticize what the pastor has exaggerated or what he should have said and didn't. And woe to him if, giving in to weariness after walking up and down the mule tracks, he has repeated himself in the sermon and surreptitiously added the conclusion of an old one. The community has the right to his new sermons

5 The word *barba*, from the Latin *barbanus*, or uncle, was a term of respect for the Waldensian preachers. The diminutive *barbetto* or *barbetti* was a popular term referring to the Waldensians.

and, in the end, the "minister" doesn't plow, doesn't milk, and doesn't hoe.

The tremendous God of my mother's forebears is the same one who compels Abraham to sacrifice his son, and who punishes with the rod of his wrath those whom He himself has chosen. And when he grants us times of peace—the usual thirty years, and if it's longer it means that in the middle of it he'll send a plague—we have to stand up to the papists and wear ourselves out in contests of virtue to prove that we're better.

At first glance it might not appear difficult: the Catholics, in fact, are very ignorant. Hadn't a Catholic girl (not from the valleys) asked me if the Waldensians were Christians? She had appeared skeptical even about the existence of the Bible. I considered the Catholics at best brothers who were wrong.

Grandfather called his worst students the philistines. They were almost all Catholics, and Grandfather was supposed to teach them French all over again, which he did, with some impatience but with a spirit of justice; in fact, he was called *le juste*, as well as *le fléau* (the scourge).

The Catholics—"Look out!"— snare souls by dishonest means. Honest means, which can be summed up in the usual "solid reasoning," are unworkable with Catholics. Of course, it would be nice to find a Catholic to reason with, but unfortunately their ignorance is a wall that can't be breached by any attempt at or temptation to reasoning.

Still, the *barbetto* God has given us this impossible task, along with these valleys to cultivate. He provides for hailstorms on the fields of the wicked and makes the vines of the good prosper, unless one fine morning he discovers they're guilty of some transgression known only to him. But terrible as he is, you have to speak to him face-to-face, and so maybe you fear the prince less—"our natural prince"—and can remind him that he arrived here after us, who have been here from time immemorial. The prince is solidly planted in the earth, even if it's the rocky, steep, and scrubby earth of the valleys. He should be followed and respected as the alternation of the seasons for sowing and reaping is respected, and the belly of the pregnant woman, who should be relieved of heavy burdens—but not all, because each of us has to carry some weight.

The devil, too, is, like the prince, natural, after all. The *barbetto* devil is flesh and blood, and, according to Janavel, you can shoot at him as if he were any papist. "Everyone—but especially the best shots—should have some bronze or iron bullets in order to punish the devil if he appears."

Why be surprised if, an unworthy substitute for the Lutheran devil, he was gone forever from under my bed, driven out by the garlic and rosemary fragrance of Grandmother's roasts—wasn't she worth at least as much as a sharpshooter?

When I set off to take my first communion—dressed in the Waldensian costume, with a handwoven pinafore that along with the cap had come down from Val d'Angrogna, *que dicitur Engrogna*—I was accompanied by the sound of the organ, and was moved. Swallowing the piece of bread and drinking the wine from the small cup, I promised God generically to be good and to suffer in silence, something that was becoming increasingly difficult for me, partly because no one cared at all that I was suffering in silence, and I missed the audience that every adult had by rights when he suffered in silence.

I didn't think about Jesus Christ; I sought in particular to avoid the thought of his death. A terror of death pursued me; I dreamed I'd be buried alive under Grandfather's vineyard in the grass, and I tried to console myself with the hope of resurrection. Despite the small certainty gained that morning in the gym, I continued to consider myself a Christian.

My sister, who a year after me refused to take first communion, reproached me for my duplicity: I was unfaithful by nature, my denials weren't decisive enough, my assents hesitant. Sisi had gone to catechism, which, she says, was held at seven in the morning, before school. She had gone, she claims, to prove that she wasn't as lazy as everyone said. Her ultimate rejection wasn't considered disgraceful; it was more disgraceful to be lazy.

As for me, what persuaded me hadn't been only my duplicity—which in some cases branched out into many more than two motivations—and my love of ritual, when the symbolism was performed well (I even liked parading around the stadium in the uniform of *giovane italiana*, carrying the pennant), but the usual contradictory desire to be like others and at the same time the best. I courted institutions and wasn't opposed in principle, but I needed time to get used to a place, and, without intending to, would stick out at the least opportune moments.

When the gym teacher shouted from the rostrum at all the schools gathered in almost perfect order on the playing field—we were in the provinces, and "almost perfect" was allowed—in their black-and-white stripes: "Who has raised her head to look around? Gersoni naturally!" Gersoni was, unfortunately, me and not my sister.

It wasn't that I rejected institutions but that institutions rejected me.

Once—it seems to me that we were already in high school—we went on an excursion to Tredici Laghi, by way of Val d'Angrogna. It's one of the ancient routes from Val Pellice to Val San Martino, and it's a long hike.

The valley starts off suddenly narrow, and at first the road follows the stream, the Angrogna. On the left, across the stream, the slope is steep and wooded. On the right you ascend, crossing small plateaus where there are villages. The main village, deep in the upper valley, is Pra del Torno. As in other high, narrow Waldensian valleys the contrast between the sunny inhabited part and the thickly wooded opposite side is intense.

We had left in the afternoon, and at sunset, a little beyond Vaccera, we asked a thickset, brown-haired mountain man who was leading his cows to their barn if we could shelter for the night. He asked us where we came from, and our name, then he pointed to the hayloft. As we entered, he looked at me and uttered a brief sentence (which I didn't understand) in his dialect, with the broad *a*'s between closed *e*'s. He then translated it into French: *"Nous sommes cousins; le professeur*

Coïsson était mon cousin."[6] He didn't say anything else, and let us into the barn.

By the time we arrived in the valleys, no close relatives of Grandfather's still lived in Angrogna. Aunt Catherine had died and, shortly afterward, Aunt Madeleine, who was in France and whom Grandfather "adored," said Grandmother, who wasn't disposed to tolerate other adored women in the family.

While in my sleep I heard the cows in the stalls below us huffing, shoving, peeing, and smelled their warm odor, which reminded me of the smell of milk—which I sometimes drank fresh from a cow—I wondered how that cousin (an Odin?) had traced our relationship through my foreign surname and why he had communicated it by simply declaring it, and with those alien vowels.

I continued to think about it the next day as we hiked in the blazing sun after a freezing-cold dawn up the *ciaplé*, the stony slope, toward Tredici Laghi, the thirteen lakes that looked to me like small puddles. How distant the big lake where I picked water lilies seemed. Here everything was encased in stone, and the water, sparingly collected, although it was deep and very clear, was more the color of the stone, gray green, almost black at night, rather than the color of the sky.

Within me, besides the surprise—how could I be the cousin of that thickset, brown-haired mountain dweller whose ancient dialect I barely understood?—and the embarrassment of not knowing how to reply, a discordant echo

6 "We're cousins, Professor Coïsson was my cousin."

responded to that recognition. I placed my nailed boots on the burning rocks—always rocks—and said to myself that, centuries ago, everyone in the valley had been like that cousin, all the way back to those who in 1332, in the square in Pra del Torno, had killed the local priest, considered the inquisitor's spy. And that, confusingly, made me proud. Yet speaking of Grandfather, my mother said: "What I couldn't bear about him was his Waldensian chauvinism."

Once a year, on February 17th, when the civil emancipation granted to the Waldensians by the ruler of Savoy, Carlo Alberto, in 1848 was celebrated, a historical drama was presented in the Collegio theater, whose subject was an episode from the exploits of *Nos Pères*. The actors were for the most part high school students; I don't remember the names of the authors.

The plays were performed in costume, the words were in Italian. The Waldensians were virtuous, the Catholics bad, the prince so-so. But as far as I remember, the Catholics were exclusively those in power: priests, bishops, evil counselors, and commanders, who (with the help of God) were defeated. There were no ordinary people, or at most mute cops.

I was crazy about those shows, compensating in my own imagination for the mediocrity of the script and the production. As I sat in the packed hall waiting for the curtain to rise, the event of the year loomed behind the red drapery on the small stage.

For several days afterward I'd go around the house like a sleepwalker: I'd find myself in the toilet halfway up the stairs holding the plate of butter I was supposed to take to the cellar. I thought endlessly about what I'd seen, I mixed and incorporated it into my fantasies, and, if I put on a show in the attic with my dolls for a sparse audience—my sister and a few friends—I intuited the inadequacy of my performance, the difference between what it should have been and what it was.

In those years I got in the habit of spending hours drawing large black-and-white figures copied from paintings and sculptures. At the painting lessons I had, thanks to one of my mother's acts of justice—my sister had singing lessons—I was taught to decorate horrible little vases. I would have liked to learn to portray a person in motion.

One of those February 17th shows provided, among other things, the provocation for the worst punishment of my adolescence, worse than being slapped, which also humiliated me, worse than cutting allusions to my physical and moral failings.

One year, a few days before February 17th, in a discussion with Grandmother—the fights between us were becoming more and more frequent—I "answered back." The Waldensians had "answered back" for centuries, but in the family you weren't supposed to answer back, just as you weren't in the neighboring Catholic valleys or at Fiat or to the traffic cop.

My answers improved over the years as I deployed increasingly clever replies. I was goaded by Grandmother's own cruelty and a certain eagerness to bite that I felt as, still slightly hunched, I began to stretch out and assert myself. A clownish desire to inflict my inferiority, to transform it, was growing in me, and again the words that I had found useful for my best lies as a child came to my aid.

That time, certainly, I had the perfect response, because Grandmother was so astonished that she retreated to her room, where she began to groan in Franco-Provençal. Her groans were very loud—in spite of the season she had even opened the window—and I took refuge behind the chicken coop, truly frightened by the success of my remark. I heard her groaning from all the way across the garden, which was illuminated by the full moon, but I didn't wonder if she was really ill; I understood that it was comedy, and she was taking advantage of the moon, as if it were a spotlight, to find me, hiding and guilty behind the chicken coop.

That answer led Grandmother to forbid me to see the performance on the seventeenth. I was crushed by that, I humbled myself and, under my sister's disdainful glances, begged her, taking back not only the response in question but those past and future. Grandmother was inflexible. But that tragic February 17th was also—thank the Lord—the occasion of the only fundamental pedagogical intuition that my grandmother had regarding me. She, too, gave up the performance that she was very fond of and walked with me up and down Via Beckwith as others hurried to the theater. Through a veil of tears—I was crying shamelessly on the street—I looked at the fires lighted on Monte Vandalino and on the Rorà hill and had a presentiment that nothing could ever replace the show I would miss that night. But Grandmother's decision made a deep impression, and I remembered it forever: by staying with me she was sharing my guilt. She wasn't getting revenge, as she often appeared to be, but helping carry my burden.

She was usually a capricious, authoritarian pedagogue who seemed to want to impose her own will rather than a general rule of behavior. She was also merciless except on rare and unexpected occasions.

When it came to herself she liked to recount the wrongs she'd suffered. While she described her great love—a very handsome young Catholic whom her mother, the Huguenot, hadn't let her marry, and who had become the stationmaster in Bricherasio, so she'd see him from the windows of the train as it went by—and recalled the insults she'd endured from her Angrogna sisters-in-law, her eyes would fill with tears, but immediately afterward, repeating a successful remark of her own, she laughed again. She was quick to laughter and tears, which made both short-lived, and gave the impression that, between a laugh and a cry, she was a woman always present to herself and very self-confident.

She talked about Grandfather, ever with tears in her eyes: *"Tu sais, moi j'étais gaie et lui était toujours triste!"*[7] or, alluding to his conjugal demands (he was ten years older than she) when both were no longer young, she said to me with a quick sob: *"C'était dur, tu sais!"*[8]

---

7 "You know, I was cheerful and he was always sad!"
8 "It was hard, you know!"

When I got my period for the first time—I had jumped down from the wall at the end of the lawn and right afterward noticed I had blood in my underpants—I ran to the house. She was in her bedroom, I explained—pleased—what had happened, and she opened her wardrobe and took a cotton diaper from a pile, evidently ready, gave it to me, taught me to put it on with safety pins, and then with sudden tears in her eyes said: *"Et bien, ma pauvre, ça commence!"*[9]

She cultivated her flower and vegetable gardens passionately. At the age of eighty she got up at six in the morning to hoe. She loved flowers as much as asparagus, and in every corner of the living room were vases of flowers, arranged randomly, without thought. In winter there was nothing. I don't recall a bouquet of bought flowers, let alone a Christmas tree or a pine bough.

She'd return from the market with the shopping bag and a live chicken tied by the legs. She'd cut its throat herself at the stream—I remember the creature's brief guttural cry—and skinned rabbits. She was very good at treating the sick; she skillfully cared for Grandfather during his last serious illness. I don't remember her ever being frightened. So I didn't recognize her in her coffin: on her face was an expression of fear and surprise. Grandmother didn't believe she had to die.

She loved to travel. She came to see us in Riga with the widow's veil on her hat. She liked to go out, and never missed a Sunday service, partly because, coming home, while we ate her excellent roast, she could serve us her satire of the

---

9 "Well, my poor girl, here you go!"

sermon: nothing escaped her, a forgotten word, a stammer, a repetition. At her funeral, the minister recalled *"l'esprit un peu sec de notre chère paroissienne."*[10]

But Grandmother's wit was anything but dry. She said to Grandfather, who liked eggs but hated chickens, and didn't want any to cross his path: *"Toi, tu voudrais que les poules ne fussent que leur trou!"*[11]

As for Grandfather, she recalled with great amusement a woman from Angrogna who touched wood whenever she met him on the street. Questioned by Grandmother, the woman revealed that Grandfather—teacher at the Collegio, editor of the local newspaper *Écho des vallées*, justice of the peace, member of an association that supported the French language—belonged to a family of sorcerers. *"Ils sont nés en grognant,"*[12] Grandmother said of the inhabitants of Angrogna, where *grognant* means both grumbling and growling.

At home, if she wasn't in the kitchen, where she cooked wonderfully, using an incredible number of pots and pans that someone else washed, Grandmother sat in an armchair at her small worktable, which had also come from her mother's house, and whose drawers were full of thread; here she sometimes fell asleep in the summer heat with her eyeglasses on the tip of her nose, then she woke up and knitted or mended while she read novels. She was a tireless reader of romance novels.

She was already sixty-five when we arrived in Torre Pellice, but she never seemed old to me—she lived by herself

---

10 "the slightly dry wit of our dear parishioner."
11 "You'd like it if the chickens were nothing more than their hole."
12 "They were born complaining."

until her death—since there was nothing that she couldn't do if she wanted to, no judgment that she didn't dare express; when she didn't understand a book, it was the book that was *bête* or *drôle*.

"She was an iconoclast," my mother would say of her; she couldn't forgive her for not appreciating the value of the refined gifts she brought her. Grandmother put everything on the same plane, the thin cotton dress and the costly shawl. She had sold to the junk dealer medals belonging to her own father, a volunteer with Garibaldi, and the magnificent walnut bed inherited from her parents. For her they were all worthless *vieilleries*. She had even burned in the stove—my mother said—many books from Grandfather's library.

What could I say, who at sixteen had burned my Bible in the wood-burning hot-water heater, tearing the pages out one by one? Submerged in the bath of all those verses as if in the stifling heat of inferno, I heard Grandmother on the other side of the door calling me: *"Mais es-tu folle, Mina?"* *"C'est fini,"* [13] I answered, in reality already repenting, not the gesture, so apt for our little domestic theater, but, rather, the definitive loss of my Bible.

My battles with her—interlocutor of my adolescence and lightning rod, certainly not voluntary, for my mother—weren't battles with an angel, an unearthly presence that assails you in the half sleep of an uncertain dawn and you don't know whether it's a blazing sword from the outside or a hidden dagger within.

---

13 "Are you crazy, Mina?" "It's over."

Grandmother was a whole person—flesh and blood, like the *barbetto* devil—and, unlike Jacob, I didn't emerge from the contest injured; rather, I came out strengthened, as if that domestic theater of ours had, without my realizing it, purged me of certain bitter moods, certain malignant wastes. As an old woman I would like to have a garden where I could pick my tomatoes and taste them still warm from the sun, right next to the stem where they have a flavor of fruit and vegetables together. And eat them with bread, the good crusty bread from Torre Pellice, the best in the world.

I went only rarely to the cemetery where my mother's family tomb is, near the entrance gate.

Sometimes I went with Grandmother to bring flowers, especially so that the *catholiques*, passing by, wouldn't be able to criticize our bare tomb. An ostentatious indifference toward the cult of the dead—perhaps one of many examples to set for the Catholics—must have been among the old Waldensian customs. But we brought flowers semisecretly to the cemetery: Grandmother wasn't afraid to be unorthodox if necessary.

As I washed the vase and changed the water, I shuddered, because the smell of rotting flowers led me to think of the people buried all around me, and I was afraid of finding a skeleton on the pile of garbage outside the enclosure. Having arranged the flowers, we took a walk around the tombs, and Grandmother would stop and comment: who was inside or outside, what they had said or done. I didn't remember anything, partly because, as usual, I was indifferent to relationships, marriages, and quarrels, and partly because I was scared. All I remember is the story of how the old cemetery that used to be opposite the movie theater, where the public park is now, was moved.

And more specifically the episode of an old woman—I think her name was Gonnet—who with the help of her maid emptied her family's tomb: *"Tiens,"* she said, taking a femur, *"ça doit être l'oncle Eugène,"* and she tossed it into the woman's broad apron. *"Et ça c'est certainement la tête de la pauvre Marie. Elle avait une si petite tête."*[14]

As a result of our visits to the cemetery I developed a long-standing antipathy toward marble floors and a complete indifference to the fate of bodies. I didn't associate the dead person with the living person who had been; rather, I found him, how to put it, troublesome, disturbing, with something malicious in his face, as if he had just played a trick on the other, the living, treacherously replacing him. As if, while we're living, our dead self were growing with us, and would suddenly surprise us and take possession of us.

Fantasies that certainly wouldn't have sat well with Grandmother. She often said the cemetery she liked most was the old Catholic cemetery behind the church, on the road that went up to the fort. Above the entrance, she recalled, were the words: "Here are neither poor nor rich." She was very proud of having been born on July 14th, Bastille Day, and she always reminded us of that.

---

14 "Here, this must be Uncle Eugene." "And that is certainly poor Marie's head. She had such a small head."

However kindly disposed, she was critical of other Protestants, and often considered them a little "excessive," and she called the Salvation Army, which had a flourishing headquarters in Torre Pellice, *l'armée du chahut*, with a play of words on *chahut*, raucous noise, and *salut*, that is, salvation.

When her son, my mother's younger brother and Grandmother's favorite—she considered him better than her daughter, which in essence meant more pliable—married a Dutch Catholic in Amsterdam, where he worked at the Italian consulate, Grandmother was pleased about the marriage and welcomed her daughter-in-law. But it was important to her that their child be baptized as a Waldensian (mainly, perhaps, out of respect for Grandfather's memory), as I, the daughter of a Jew, had been. And she told me later, she had made her son swear on the family Bible that he had never given in to the enemy. The Bible, placed on a small table in the living room, was seldom used; once when the pastor was visiting—this was after Grandfather's death—and asked for it, a spider emerged frightened from between the pages, which Grandmother leafed through only when she didn't feel well (that is, had indigestion), and that didn't happen often. Still, swearing was considered a very serious act, almost unseemly, and Grandmother must have decided on it for a reason she felt was truly essential. When the Catholic daughter-in-law revealed herself in due course to be treacherous and dishonest, Grandmother left to her daughter the small lawn—"my" lawn—remaining from her dowry, provoking a series of legal complications that I had to untangle some thirty years later.

Indeed, even if the history that came to us from the mountains was shared, the inheritances were meticulously divided; I still have from one such division a big hand-woven sheet, in that impossible Calvinist, mountain size that doesn't fit a single bed or a double bed or even, very well, a three-quarter bed.

As for Uncle Robert, he'd had to choose which one he'd give in to, and his son had in fact been baptized as a Catholic. Someone in Torre Pellice observed to him as an adult: "A Catholic Coïsson!" and said no more.

Although Grandmother was oppressive in her criticisms and comments and combative in her actions, she was singularly tolerant of our friendships. She had, it's true, an infallible nose for my infatuations, which she remarked on at the table in an incisive, malicious way, but she left us free to play for hours outside the gate, to go down through the fields to the Pellice, which in summer we crossed by jumping from rock to rock. When we were older we went on excursions in the mountains and, in a group, bicycled (I was last of all to learn) down through the valley toward Bricherasio and Pinerolo. Girls and boys of our age would come to our house.

In my friendships I acted as a matchmaker or village sorcerer, according to the occasion. I fostered passionate but shadowy loyalties—I find many names in my diary—and easily felt betrayed. I would then drop the friend and retreat into sullen disappointment.

I was slowly separating from my sister. She indicated that she couldn't bear what she called my dramatic "poses" as an actress; the strange, convoluted way I approached matters; my Don Quixote-esque impulses restrained by cowardice and timidity. And I was wounded by her brutal comments, especially about my appearance. More and more often I heard her nascent beauty praised: if I liked a boy, she stole him by her mere presence, without making a move. It was precisely her impassive stillness—I kept muddling along— that crushed me. She was absorbed in her own fascination with lazy cruelty, her eyes firm, clear, full of proud ferocity.

My jealousy, as in childhood, didn't undermine the solidarity I felt with her, wasn't related solely to her—about whom my mother was silent, while her face lit up—but was a feeling I would call inevitable, deep-rooted. My defeats plunged me into a primitive melancholy, and for years any allusion to her beauty or elegance—but also to the success of anyone else—overwhelmed me with a mortal sadness that at first drove me to give up, to sink once more under the ice of the winter sea in Riga. Then I reemerged and got busy again.

I gave my friends advice, I listened to their confidences (the disappointed lovers of my sister, who was very selective, came to tell me their romantic sufferings), sometimes I exchanged one confidence for another, but mainly I was investigating myself, what people thought of me.

I furtively read letters that were written at home; I tried to apprehend conversations by surprise. I was always sure I'd find flattering appreciations of myself when I picked up a letter left unguarded on the table. And if instead of praise I found negative judgments, which was what usually happened, I enjoyed those, too, as they supported my position as "serenely solitary." The phrase is from my diary, where I find it already in ironic quotation marks.

I was twenty when, going into my mother's room one day, I saw a letter on the desk, complete with salutation and signature, written in her beautiful clear handwriting. Even now the sight of any sample of her writing moves me, as if I had a more intimate relation with her writing than with her.

In that period, with the war over, theatrical performances resumed. I had been given an important part in a play, a comic-pathetic role. Overcoming my terror of being onstage, I'd had a genuine success. Someone had even stopped me on the street the next day to congratulate me.

So the letter lay on the desk, surely full of enthusiastic praise for me; I began to read, and found instead a long, insistent—a good half page—description of my sister, who as an extra in another play had crossed the stage fleetingly in white wig and Goldonian costume and, turning her head somewhat awkwardly toward the audience, had asked, with her slightly defective pronunciation of s: "But where is the baroness?"

Standing straight in front of the desk, with the letter in my hand, I was agitated by disappointment, triumph (I've got you, stupid, you with the favoritism you always deny), and above all dismay. The tone of enchantment with which my mother wrote about my sister, the effusiveness so different from her habitual reticence, seemed to me unnatural and forbidding. No optimism could overcome that pitiless confirmation.

Her usual exaggerated refusal to praise me was natural—
she was educating me—but the brutal innocence with which
she obliterated me from the page, denying me any hope, was
monstrous.

Suddenly, when I left the room—whom could I tell
without also disclosing my indiscretion?—an ironic sneer,
in quotation marks, surprised me, like a surge of joy: there
is always some secret to discover in the heart and soul of
others. Alas.

Gradually I stopped glancing at other people's letters. I
still like reading books of letters and diaries, though; maybe
that's how I satisfy a lingering Peeping Tom curiosity.

Withdrawing to enjoy my "serene solitude," I read and
fantasized a lot. During vacations I might not go beyond the
gate for weeks. In summer I was allowed to stay alone in the
little room under the gabled roof. While I settled with my
books into the warm dusty odor of the wooden walls, I was
torn between the satisfaction of being able to lock myself in
and revulsion toward the swifts that made nests all around.
I heard them arrive, beating their wings, landing with heavy
thuds, and I considered whether it might not be better to
confront the daily fights with Sisi in our shared room. But
the nights, fragrant with hay, sparkling with stars, immense
over my head as I looked out the little attic window, filled me
with rapture. I felt gigantic energies in myself, still held tight,
it's true, in the grip of my will, not dissolved and soothed in
the flow of a true presentiment but ready for flight.

I fantasized for hours walking back and forth on the

balcony—in winter on the first-floor landing—and the heroine of my fantasies was very beautiful. Very handsome, too, was the hero, with whom I identified just as fervently.

But what transported me on summer nights beyond the dark mass of the mountains and the unceasing roar of the river was the approach of a reality that I feared and tried to insulate myself from. I wrote in my diary: "I'm afraid of the woman that I'm about to become, that I will fatally become if nothing interrupts the necessary evolution of my spiritual life. I feel her already alive in me, and every day she becomes more mature and complete."

Group excursions to the mountains gave me the same sensation of being stirred at once by fear and avidity. After crossing the last fields, I took my bare feet out of the boots to rest on the short, coarse, fragrant grass of where we stopped. We climbed toward long rocky crests, hardened by sun and frost. They were our peaks, and they all resembled one another. The stones slid under our feet toward the gullies below. I was usually among the first to arrive and among the last on the descent: my ankles, barely protected by the edge of the boots, couldn't support my long legs, and I was constantly wrenching them on the way down.

For me all goals were the same. Violent thoughts agitated me during the hike and sometimes became emotions: arriving among the first, descending among the last, talking to the boy I was in love with, but always life, with birth and death, and I, what was I doing there. As if the sun-soaked stones crumbling under my boots into increasingly fine fragments as we neared the peak were one of those symbols that I was fascinated to see represented.

Talking to my mother in old age I tried to retrace the routes of these excursions, but apart from the mountains I didn't recognize the places, the villages, the pastures, the lake. She traveled around there with ease, that village was such and such, in that other she had stayed with her father, who was taking her on a hike and had taught her to beat the ground with a stick to chase away the vipers. She cited names not only with infallible geographic precision (the Angrognine vowels accurately pronounced) but also as the names of real places, roads, bridges, each different from the others and in each a memory different from the others.

For me memory was singular, bare and hard like the stony ground: the need I had for others—to pass them walking, give them a hand, talk to them, touch them—and my inferiority to them.

I wrote in my diary: "I need to exert my personality over others either in opposition when I can't dominate them or in friendships where I'm the stronger."

I returned from excursions the way one returns from a defining adventure, and as I dragged my aching feet along the final kilometers, I often fell into a deep depression: yet again I hadn't managed to join in.

To tell the truth, there was no gap between my fantasies and the fulfillment of a reality both feared and desired but, at best, opposition between my ambitions and the implacability that was a condition of their success.

Still, after all, the force and intensity with which I portrayed life (and enjoyed portrayals of life) and the force and intensity with which I lived and tried to assert myself were both drives of my ego, and not only didn't fight but coexisted without schizoid torment or twin-like adhesion. Already as a child I was carried away by the beauty of the lies I invented but never confused with reality, and similarly, later, I would put on my different pairs of boots in turn, now going seven leagues, now only two inches; but the huge seven-league leap didn't suffer from the extreme patience of my two inches.

The parallel existence of practicality and imagination that was congenial to me complicated my relations with others; I would have liked to be accepted in my wholeness, and I continued to be surprised each time—and so I isolated myself—that to be accepted I had to reduce, confine, castrate myself. Maybe that's why it seemed to me that I found unity in performing. And was, besides, entirely likable at last.

Inevitably, however, now and then I would be seized by a nostalgia for reunion (for "return," I say to myself, and yet again this *Sehnsucht*, yearning, becomes a liturgical nostalgia for a return to the immense luminous beach of childhood), and not only that, but I shaped as privilege and named as choice the yearned-for truce.

I started writing relatively late. At first I wrote some poems, only two of which I've saved. I kept a diary to narrate myself to myself. When I was eighteen it was considered unseemly to have, for whatever reason, psychological difficulties (the word wasn't used; in a letter to my mother I find "psychic"); we don't talk about anyone who might have suffered from the notorious "nervous exhaustion." Worse than syphilis. Preoccupation with oneself, reflecting on one's own conflicts, was the sign of an equivocal and, naturally, weak character.

Also at eighteen I started writing a play with a friend. At that time I was overcome by a general nausea toward reading. In the preceding years I had read through Grandfather's library—almost all the books were in French—and whatever books or pages I happened to come upon. Grandmother, who had exiled Zola to the top shelf, considering it dangerous (I read *Nana* standing on the threshold of her room, not having yet discovered the use of the flashlight to illuminate banned books under the covers at night), gave me romance novels that my mother considered repulsive. She let me read any book, provided it was by an important author, a "good" book. I remember reading *Les Dames Galantes*, by Brantôme, from beginning to end, curled up in front of the lighted stove in her room during a Christmas sojourn. I greeted a toothache that arrived at the end of the reading as the well-deserved divine punishment.

So between the prohibitions of the two of them I read every readable book in the house, apart from the many volumes of geography. Reading, I discovered that Don Carlos had a hunchback; it was an unpleasant discovery, since I still couldn't bear the hunchbacks of History. I also found in an autopsy report on Napoleon that he had small genital organs. I was ignorant of everything on the subject, having missed, because of the long-ago betrayal of my Finnish friend, the chance to find out, while I knew a lot, from *Les Dames Galantes*, about the measure of females. But I saw a kind of disappointment, and surprise, in the statement that such a great man had small genitals, that he wasn't "handsome," in other words. Anyway, I didn't love Napoleon—I loved Athos—nor did I love Louis XIV or Alexander the Great.

I was attracted by the great confusion of peoples, by the fanfares, by the cavalry galloping in the night, by the crowd gathered in the cathedral to sing the Te Deum, by the tumult that accompanied and surrounded their appearance, by the *remue-ménage*, the commotion, Grandmother, who liked to denigrate anyone, and especially great men, would have said. I didn't mind seeing the great man in a nightcap as long as it could be demonstrated that even in a nightcap he deserved fanfares and bows. And I was divided between hatred for the Grande Armée swallowed up by the Russian snow and admiration for the French *pontonniers*, submerged in the frigid Berezina, whose ceaseless repairs allowed their companions to flee over the wooden bridge. I could never stay decisively on one side, for the conquerors soon became the conquered and I had to change flags.

I read Jules Verne, but the geography didn't interest me; maybe I was convinced that it could have easily been invented. Besides, didn't I always wander around unknown cities with the topographical intuition of the one who had planned and built them himself?

The rhythm of the wheels of a train at night still takes me back to childhood sensations: plains, mountains, rivers; the lights of stations where the noise of the journey pauses. The cities I arrive in and depart from are always a station; as the train passes, mountains, rivers, plains become anonymous, and down there behind the lighted windows you see others in their precarious and illusory immobility, for they, too, are on the train traveling with me.

No, I didn't care about maps, banal surrogates for invention. Or more simply I rejected the change, the transmutation, out of a kind of laziness, the same that had surprised me as I learned one language after another, and had prevented me from recognizing the name of the *Römer* so obvious in that of the Romans.

Every language had qualities that were neither translatable nor interchangeable. In every language I was different. Every language has its time.

I recall the terrible feeling of impotence I had once during the first months in Torre Pellice, when, on the ground floor of the house, I met a worker who asked for Grandmother; I understood the meaning of the question, but I wasn't capable of explaining that Grandmother was upstairs, in her room. The words lay dead in my mouth, I was paralyzed between one life and the other.

For some years no language seemed to me especially beautiful; all languages were useful. And later, when I became accustomed to the school use of Italian and began to have fun with my compositions (although I always had doubts about spelling and syntax, having learned French and Italian almost at the same time), I was limited, I would say, by a lack of inner connection to the technical means of the language: for example, I could never recite an Italian poem perfectly, despite my good memory. Sometimes I realized that one sentence flowed better than another, but I didn't know why.

I remember clearly when I understood that words placed in a certain order—following an absolute necessity—were beautiful. Rereading Schiller's *Don Carlos* yet again (I read and reread the books that affected me, I carried them with me everywhere, I didn't care about the name of the author and savagely skipped the pages that didn't interest me)—anyway, reading *Don Carlos* again, in the school edition that my mother, studying to be a teacher, had used at the university, I came to where the prince sees Elisabeth for the last time and says to her, *"So sehen wir uns wieder."*[15] I repeated the phrase and was moved. I heard a small pause after the *So* and the lengthening toward death of the final *wieder*. I was moved not because the prince was about to die—a standard occurrence in a play—but by the inevitability with which the words were joined together and separated, *those* words and in *that* way.

Then Italian had its moment: late, in fact. Of my school texts I remember rereading the duel of Tancredi and Clorinda, and the end of *The Prince*, several times. Only when, as a university student, I heard Pastonchi recite Canto XXVI of the *Inferno* did I have a flash of understanding about Dante.

I read and reread the *Canti* of Leopardi, which had been given to me by a young student who had tutored us in Latin

---

15 "So we meet again."

during middle school, because my mother was afraid that we wouldn't keep up. For years this student, who was much older than I was, already a young man when I was twelve, wrote me long letters that I threw in the stove. He had a faithful admiration for me, but, even though I so much wanted to be admired, I felt very uneasy about it, because, as always, the mere suspicion that someone might fall in love with me, unreciprocated, instilled terror and embarrassment, as if I were facing incest.

Italian was therefore the Esperanto in which I began to write. That first play was historical, like the ones that were performed on February 17th, like the plays of Schiller. It took place in Spain during the Inquisition, among Protestants and Catholics. There was a lot of dialogue, and everyone was very witty, even the cops, the Protestants slightly more than the Catholics.

In the meantime I had started going to the movies on Sunday afternoons, and my passion for spectacle was fueled decisively. The cinema not only left its sediments but seemed to stir the depths of my imagination and bring to light buried correlations and images. It set in motion my imaginative world, opened pathways, unexpected approaches, oblique references I hadn't thought of before.

So when the play was finished, the notion of a film on Waldensian history came to mind. I was goaded polemically toward that island whose narrow-mindedness and pettiness I hated; I wanted to argue a little with the church Fathers, talk back, make them get off their pedestals. On the other hand the perfection of their story stimulated me, a perfection that seemed to reflect a requirement of my own that I didn't care to acknowledge.

I got the idea for the project reading an essay published by the Society for Waldensian Studies on the Glorious Return;[16] in it I'd found, among other things, the names of two victims of 1686, Madeleine and Catherine Coïsson, like Grandfather's sisters. That renewed echo of the Angrognino cousin's greeting certainly played a role in my inspiration. The film would have to be a Western, in which, in the end, the good win out over the bad, but it remained among the few notes of that time; and when, at twenty-one, I left the valleys I didn't give it a thought until one night thirty years later, at dinner on the Po with friends. There was talk of the Waldensians, and my film project unexpectedly returned to mind.

As I was telling the story of the forebears who, on hands and knees, holding on to each other by the pants, escaped at night from the enemy surrounding them on Balsiglia and whispered a curse on the young cook who dropped the pot that bounced from rock to rock among the tents of the sleeping Frenchmen, I realized I had forgotten nothing. As if the *barbetto* God, leaping down without warning from the Val d'Angrogna, had been hiding in my mind, fermenting, like wine in a barrel. Every image was still there, fresh, whole, invented just yesterday.

---

16 In 1689, a group of Waldensians returned from exile and reconquered their homelands; this was referred to as the Glorious Return, or *La Glorieuse Rentrée*.

I hadn't returned to Torre Pellice except for brief periods right after my marriage and occasional visits later. The house had been divided between my mother and my uncle, and the part that was my mother's had remained uninhabited. The lawn had lost some pear and apple trees, the big cherry tree near the gate—there was a smaller one a little farther along—the fig tree where I read, imagining I was on the deck of a sailboat, and the grass below the wave-filled ocean. Houses had been built all around, and a little beyond the lawn's boundary wall ran the noisy ring road, where once fields had stretched to the Pellice.

Besides, I had only seldom, and only on the basis of very precise reminders, thought back to my adolescence and youth; my childhood—which had now become history and, as it seemed, detached from me—had, on the contrary, stayed with me while I had children and brought them up. The disorderly pile of later periods I had pushed away like a jumbled mass in which I could barely isolate the date of my marriage, the birth of the children, the moves. Not even the years when I had taught in this or that school: every time I had to fill out documents, I had to start from the beginning and count and check. My excellent memory was useful only for the written page, the image seen and the one invented.

When I happened to reread my diary or the letters to my mother that I had managed to retrieve, I seemed to perceive conspiratorial winks above my adolescent self, as if two plotters were confronting each other between the lines; each knew something about the other that could have embarrassed him and each was silent out of his own self-interest.

Perhaps I had the sensation that events—happiness and unhappiness commented on and noted—were in fact within the category of the inessential; that the essential was to reveal itself later. Was this the secret that the two plotters were winking at?

I remember the first time I said to myself: I'm happy. I was seventeen and was running down across the lawn. It was May or early July—the grass was still short or had already been cut—and suddenly for the first time the future filled me: Aldo was about to return from Rome (today you'd say my boyfriend, but at the time there was no name to indicate aloud the beloved). Summer was waiting for me, long, interminable; in Grandmother's garden I sometimes secretly kissed the soft, perfumed laps of the roses.

But both happiness and unhappiness were only scratches on a smooth surface: in reality, nothing penetrated the depths of the amoeba it covered. Events were crushed against it, were absorbed, transformed, digested, and allowed the formless inner being to expand and contract according to its own rules and needs.

Of wartime I remember the autumn days in Torre, the evenings with dogs barking in the dark countryside, and the fog that smelled of the stoves lighted in the houses. Or very clear days in March, when there were no shadows in the garden, and, at the end of the valley, the sky animated by both sun and wind above the mountains.

In my entire diary only two dates refer to the events of those years; maybe the uneasiness I feel in rereading it, and the reluctance to remember, lies in those limitations of my memory, as, during the wait for reality, every feeling that wasn't the feeling of myself dissolved. I was at a standstill on the threshold of myself.

Only anger and pity truly agitated me to the depths, both incongruous pseudopods of the amoeba I was talking about before.

I felt a vigilant but labile pity—stingy like the liking I felt for myself and nourished precisely by my feeling of inferiority—toward anyone who was for any reason mocked and persecuted by others, by the strong. I seldom dared to show my pity.

And so for the young substitute literature teacher, Catholic, a nephew of the bishop of Pinerolo, summoned to teach in the middle school here—for lack of anything better—the Liceo-Ginnasio of Torre Pellice. Thin, pale, with slightly reddened eyelids.

One morning he asked one of my classmates, a broad, robust country girl from San Giovanni who even then was planning to be a midwife, what the Madonna of Dresden in a photo in our anthology made her think of. And she, rising tranquilly, in a clear, sonorous voice had answered: "Of an idol."

In the roar of laughter that followed this answer—laughter that might have appeared to be directed at the innocent country girl but was instead directed at him, the papist, who believed he could provoke, but had been shot—I seemed to perceive behind the reddened eyelids two tears and, oh, how I would have liked to find a consoling response and the courage to offer it. Yet not only did the Madonna of Dresden not inspire me but along with pity for the bishop of Pinerolo's nephew I felt some disgust for him, so ugly, so thin and pale.

Those I pitied often slightly disgusted me. Thus the poor man with the Waldensian surname, a peasant from the hill in Torre Pellice, who promised cigarettes to my male classmates in exchange for "appointments."

One of them had confided this to me; they also told me about going in a group on bicycles to a brothel in Pinerolo, and boasted of coming home "so weak they could barely hold on to the handlebars."

I received these confidences without batting an eye. I found it despicable that they got the cigarettes in advance from that poor man, who then waited for them behind a bush—here, too, they went in a group—and having got the cigarettes they followed him home shouting insults and throwing stones. He fled, begging for mercy, afraid that someone in his family would hear them. As for the service that they were supposed to perform—and which they dishonestly refused—I didn't exactly understand what it was. Besides, although I was curious, I didn't dare find out: sex was something gross, a damp and sticky touching, expelling and receiving liquids, being insulted and stoned. Nothing that happened to me seemed yet to be part of it. Not the little trick invented by my sister that in our private language had the German name *das Schöne*, not the sudden jolt in my groin when the boy who was chasing me in fun suddenly grabbed me, not even my lengthy fantasies.

My senses didn't sleep, they dreamed, curbed by the sheer intensity of the dreams rather than by the restraints of upbringing and the times. Sometimes they awoke unexpectedly at the warm contact of even an unknown arm, or at the sudden direct glance of someone I'd never noticed. But I was too attached to absolute requirements of beauty—beauty of action—to follow such calls.

In my diary the date of June 20th is repeated for three years, the day in 1943 I fell in love with the person I find later designated only by the initial "A."

I had been in love before and would be later; this love, however, repeated on three dates, had a particular importance because it pushed me to confront myself with myself for the first time. It was the primary motivation for keeping my diary in a sustained way. Of course, put like that, it excludes him, my "A.," hurling him into the disembodied world of my phantoms, and even less reproduces the intense fragrance of the winter air, a shining day in December when we stopped to rest in the midday sun on the roof of a hut just emerging from the snow. Yet that love left me as completely as the sand dries after a violent summer storm. Not because it wasn't at the time very strong and painful— long-lasting and not reciprocated—but because it released nothing in my inner self except the awkward and sometimes lucid lines of my diary. It still belonged completely to the inner storytelling that kept me in adolescence beyond the usual limits before I began to write. It was precisely the smell of the winter air and the sound of a Chopin nocturne played by Giuseppe, rather than a recognized surge of the senses, and, as such, it, too, always led me back to myself. I could perhaps say that it was the first, somewhat frigid attempt to love myself.

I quoted: *"Ce n'est pas un amour, l'amour trouve sa fin dans un acte; c'est une nostalgie, c'est avoir le mal d'un être comme on a le mal d'un pays. Et ceci est sans remède."* [17]

On June 5, 1944, I wrote in my diary, "Rome has fallen. And German soldiers defended it!" Four more exclamation points follow, along with a Latin quotation (I was studying the complete works of Horace for the Latin literature exam), then "Where are the Italians? On the battlefields in Africa, Russia, Greece. The Italians of Italy have betrayed their homeland. Only the dead were true Italians."

Two weeks later, I was bicycling with my friend Giorgio, returning from Pinerolo, where we had gone to get the plans of the city's barracks. Giorgio had put these plans, which were on rather big sheets of paper, in his pocket. I pedaled beside him because my presence was intended to make him appear more natural at various roadblocks we had to pass. He had with him a document exempting him from military service as a Waldensian student of theology.

It wasn't clear to me why I was there. But I wasn't worried

---

17 "This is not love, love finds its end in an act; it's nostalgia, it's feeling homesick for a being as one feels homesick for a country. And this has no cure."

about it. Giorgio and I had plenty to talk about, and I was happy to try starting a little argument with him.

At home we were too immersed in our internal conflicts to pay attention to external ones. Grandmother considered wars the useless and damaging occupation of great men. My mother's joke-telling antifascism irritated me; I knew she had been fascist in 1920, one of the first Fascist Party members in Genoa, where she was teaching at the time, and I found in her a certain fatuousness. I didn't know the whole earlier history of antifascism; Grandmother told me that Grandfather would slip away in a hurry when he met a group of fascist boys, not only because he abhorred fascism but so as not to have to salute those armed brats.

She had also told me that when at the armistice of 1918 the maid rushed into the house shouting that the war was over, and everyone had gone to the square to celebrate, he wouldn't go out: he hadn't wanted the war and now he didn't intend to celebrate the bloody victory.

Grandmother, naturally, was a republican; I was torn between a secret love for Peter of Yugoslavia (photographed in a white uniform behind his father's bier) and disgust for the incomprehensible devotion of many Waldensians to the inelegant Savoys. They even boasted that the royals preferred Waldensian maids to all others.

The practices of fascism—fascist Saturdays, compositions on the Duce, gymnastic exercises—had greeted me in Italy accompanied by the widespread, saccharine sound of "Faccetta nera," the marching song of the regime. At the same time I was met with an entire, completely new series of customs that I couldn't distinguish at all as different from the fascist ones. Everything for me was "Italian." But since in the Waldensian world the important celebrations were, somehow or other, on February 17th and August 15th, when a great collective walk celebrated *La Glorieuse Rentrée*, those anniversaries ended up being much more significant for me than the imported October 28th.[18]

But mass demonstrations, especially in films, were pleasing to my theatrical tastes. The closer authority was to me, the more unjust it seemed; as it got further away it acquired the dignity and weight of a moral entity. I was inclined to obey and considered that obedience neither more nor less than one of those prices adults had always made me pay, so that—once duty was done—I could retreat to a corner to do my own business. I felt a little guilty—a little cowardly—when I took refuge in my corners; so I considered it an act of virtue to be dragged to a torchlight procession to celebrate the taking of Barcelona or to go to the Saturday afternoon assembly.

Mussolini was therefore simply the State, in my eyes, recipient of fanfares and bows: a state that unfortunately had a potbelly and made many grimaces, grimaces that every so often provoked laughter, quickly muffled, during newsreels at the cinema. That bothered me, like my mother's jokes, even if deep down I found the goose-stepping Italians basically ridiculous.

---

18 On October 28, 1940, Mussolini announced that Italian troops had invaded Greece.

For the still more distant Hitler I felt a kind of repugnance: his shrieked speeches, his way of being German didn't at all correspond to the idea of German I had been brought up with.

Once, at fifteen, I happened to win the *Ludi Juveniles*, the fascist youth competition, in Torre Pellice with an essay on I no longer remember what. I went to get the prize—*The Story of San Michele*, by Axel Munthe—at the local fascist headquarters, I think in the elementary school. I was led into a small bare room where the young fascist in charge in Torre Pellice was to give me the book. He was scarcely more than a kid, pale, with very light blue eyes against his white skin, and well known as a staunch ideologue. He picked up the book and, observing my face with his faraway eyes, praised me briefly for the essay, then asked, abruptly, what was my fascist faith. Just like that. My fascist faith. Now, I've already said that as a rule I tried to adapt (when I wasn't gripped by a raging fury), and I desperately sought a valid response, but nothing came to mind and I was silent. He then shrugged his shoulders and locked his lips in a bitter crease. With the same bitter crease—I imagine—he died, battered by the crowd in front of the Porta Nuova station in the last days of April, 1945, at the end of the war, when Turin was liberated.

In my memory of the encounter a faint sensation of pity lingers, not the sort that overwhelmed me: even if I had disappointed him, he was still, in his thin boots, on the side of the stronger. I had felt the same faint sensation toward the very timid and cultured vice principal of the Liceo-Ginnasio

Valdese, to whom, by law, I had had to bring a declaration
of mixed race or of non-Aryan race—I don't remember the
terms—and who, red in the face and very embarrassed (I
think he had been a student of Grandfather's), had had, by
law, to take it.

The morning of July 25, 1943, I had awakened early
and gone to the living room to secretly listen to the radio.
I was therefore the first in the house to learn of the fall of
Mussolini; but when I communicated the fact to my mother
and grandmother, I wasn't believed: I was capable of invent-
ing even the end of the world. I had my revenge a few minutes later when the radio repeated the news. My mother, in
nightgown and slippers, rushed into the street shouting: "It's
over, it's over. He's fallen!"

I was outraged and incredulous and no less outraged two
months later when, on September 8th,[19] people ransacked
the barracks and I met a girl who was notoriously rich—and
Waldensian—with a pair of skis over her shoulder, on the
street that led from the barracks to the town. Behind her,
Sergio Toja, who was later the first to die as a partisan, was
pushing a wheelbarrow full of weapons.

At night, he brought the same wheelbarrow to our house,
where, unknown to Grandmother, we buried the weapons
in the cellar. I can't reconstruct through what intermedi-
ary we made the arrangement for this operation; I scarcely
knew Sergio, who was two years older than I was. We also

19 In July of 1943 Mussolini and the Fascist government collapsed; on September 8th
  Italy officially surrendered to the Allies and the Germans occupied the country from
  Rome north.

hid under the roof tiles some issues of Alberto's underground newspaper *Giustizia e Libertà*, which seemed very important to him but which I never read.

I found the whole thing incongruous, I couldn't see connections between events that didn't correspond to my usual readings of History, which corresponded, instead, to cheering crowds and orderly armies.

Again it seemed very strange—and not to say outrageous—that, also on September 8th, Grandmother dressed some "deserting" soldiers in civilian clothes belonging to Grandfather and my uncle. And not even in the house. She gave them the garments and made them strip to their underpants on the small ledge behind the clematis.

I had in the meantime met an anti-fascist, my Italian teacher, the pastor Francesco Lo Bue, whose nickname, Franchi, I used later when I spent time with him. We knew he was being watched.

I studied him attentively when he slowly turned his back to the class and looked outside, while the radio was obliged to transmit some special announcement.

With the same impassivity, long beard, absent gaze, lost, perhaps, in the previous night's drinking (he sometimes still smelled of it) or in his theological studies, he came into the classroom and passed unhurriedly under our arms raised in the fascist salute.

Our slow pace irritated me—in February, in the first year of high school, we were still occupied with St. Francis, writing down the observations that Lo Bue dictated to us—but I felt a kind of respect for that slow pace: it was my first encounter with a high quality of study and an indifference toward time. I also felt, although he gave no particular signal, attention focused on me. In a long comment appended to the grade on an essay on the poet Cecco Angiolieri, in which he pointed out that my opinion had already been expressed, with greater critical skill, however, by the literary critic Francesco Flora (whom we didn't know), the word "skill" replaced "sensibility," which he had written first and then erased. That erasure was the first literary recognition I received.

In the meantime the resistance had begun in our valleys. One of the founding groups was launched, purely by chance, at our house, on Vicolo Dagotti.

We rented a room to a young man, the boyfriend of Marisa, our neighbor and contemporary. He was a grown man—and so I judged Marisa's choice odd—an officer in the Alpine troops. Entering his room with the tea tray, I found him with two other men; they had unfolded a big map of the valley on the bed and were marking points with a pencil. I connected the map and the little circles to conversations and comments, and thus, in that room full of cigarette smoke, I saw for the first time—and was incredulous and not part of it—adults disobeying.

One morning some months later, I met, with the same sense of alienation, as if it were something that didn't concern me, Lo Bue coming up from the town, staggering. I thought he was drunk. He stopped me and said:

"You know Sergio is dead?"

"I know," I said. I was a little worried about the weapons buried in the cellar. My Dutch aunt—who didn't know about them—every day threatened to report us because of our Jewish father and our friends. I wondered who would come to get them now that Sergio was dead. I felt not sorrow for his death but that bewildered sense of guilt you have as a young person when someone your age dies.

Not knowing what to say to Lo Bue, I said goodbye and set out toward the town. As I went on, an intuition slowly began to take shape in me: Franchi wasn't drunk; he was swaying because he was desperate. He was reproaching himself because it was his own teaching that had led Sergio to his death. Ridiculous reproaches, I said to myself, each of us is responsible for ourself at whatever age. But in front of Franchi, who was reeling as if he had been hit along with Sergio, I felt again a kind of respect. In that staggering I glimpsed, in fact, the despair of true pity, what was still denied to me, since I continued to feel compassion only for those with whom I could identify.

I disapproved of the mad undertaking in which Sergio had lost his life. At the time I disapproved of almost all the partisan enterprises in our valley, at least the ones I knew about. I found them disorganized, disorderly, pointlessly dangerous. When Franchi explained to me that their intention was to contain the Germans on another front, I thought—and told him—of the disproportion between the efficiency and number of the Germans and the chaotic paucity of the partisans.

There was a rumor in Torre Pellice that the only ones who

were well trained and sufficiently armed were the Garibaldini of Luserna—the communists. I don't know if it was because they really were or if it was in comparison with Giustizia e Libertà. My friends were all in the Giustizia e Libertà groups, so I didn't know anything precise about the Garibaldini of Luserna. They were talked about as people completely without scruples, textile-factory workers, Russian deserters, and soldiers from the south who had remained trapped in Piedmont, but that didn't outrage me; scruples were an obstacle to action that I myself, however, faced only in theory. I found atrocious the execution of a fascist family in Torre Pellice (supposedly at the hands of Giustizia e Libertà)—an execution that angered everyone. But although the brutality of the act repelled me, I was tempted to consider logical the fact that the woman who might have been able to provide the names of the perpetrators was killed in her hospital bed by unknown assassins.

I considered that rich girl carrying off the skis reprehensible and equally reprehensible the useless risk, the waste of life; seeing a gurney carrying newborns passing by in the corridor of a maternity ward, I feel content, as if I were looking at the display window of a bakery. It would never even occur to me to have an abortion.

When the Germans (specifically the Austrian Alpenjäger) arrived in Torre Pellice, and, crouching in the attic at Marisa's house, I saw them, from the dormer window, passing on the street in their trucks on the way to carry out a roundup in the valley, sitting motionless one beside the other, machine guns between their legs, I sensed an enormous distance between us. They sat in the open trucks, their backs slightly curved, impassive as gray sacks of cement. I didn't recognize the world they came from, certainly it wasn't that of Arminius and the ugly duckling—but I knew where they were going. They were going to the mountains where I had walked with friends and acquaintances, while the stones crumbled under our boots. They were going indifferent and armed. I couldn't go with them. I stayed on the other side—as usual not absolutely faithful. The absolute, in fact, remained inside me. Experience, not the absolute I held within, determined my actions—as it often did later, too.

Thus on that morning in June of 1944 I was pedaling beside Giorgio, whose pockets were bulging with maps. My job was to remember the facts that his informers—two hatters and a young man with a red beard—had provided him with. He remembered nothing and I boasted of my iron memory. But I was so inattentive to practical details—at home they assigned me the dirty work, washing dishes and watering the potatoes at the end of the lawn—that I had to be very careful not to confuse the number of submachine guns with the number of machine guns, and, besides, I recognized only the thud of mortars. All other shots for me were shots.

At the bridge in Bibiana some quite young Italian soldiers stopped us. Giorgio says they were SS *rosse*—Italian SS.

They asked for our documents, but the officer who read Giorgio's exemption wasn't persuaded. He asked, in an Italian accent:

"Theology? What does that mean?"

"I'm studying to become a pastor," said Giorgio.

"Meaning what?"

"A Waldensian priest."

"And you're going around with a girl? What sort of priest!"

So they took him away. I saw him go over the bridge, on foot, pushing the bicycle, between two soldiers. They took him to Bibiana, around two kilometers away, where there was a German command. As he crossed the bridge, his pockets were bulging and looked incredibly conspicuous to me.

I leaned the bicycle against a bench and sat down. We, the Italian SS and I, were under an enormous horse chestnut tree, just at the entrance to the bridge. There was a long table with benches and, nearby, the camp kitchen.

The June day was beautiful and clear, it was around noon. My feet felt very light, a sensation not repeated since. We wore boots for eight months, and sometimes, if we slept in random shelters, we couldn't even take them off at night. The first weeks we walked in shoes, our feet, as I said, felt very light, announcing spring.

They were cooking a bean soup, and as the smell rose toward the leaves of the horse chestnut tree, the hunger of midday rose in me. The soldiers were coming and going, setting the table. I began to swallow saliva; the smell of minestrone, increasingly dense and persistent, surrounded me. Finally—more than an hour had passed since Giorgio was taken away—when they brought the pot to the table and sat down, I asked:

"Would you give me a bowl? I'm hungry."

They had me sit down and filled a metal soup plate for me. We were finishing the soup when I saw Giorgio reappear on the bridge pushing his bicycle, with the same two soldiers. His pockets appeared still to be bulging. Reaching the table, he said to me:

"Let's go. Everything's fine."

So we left on our bicycles. He pedaled in silence and I tried in vain to get him to tell me what had happened.

He told the story later, though not to me: he was taken to the barracks in Bibiana, where he was made to wait, then interrogated: who he was, where he was going, and what was the story of his document of exemption. As they were starting to raise their voices, but hadn't yet searched him, a German officer arrived—when, years later, he decided to describe the episode to me, too, he specified "a very handsome officer"—who, taking the piece of paper and seeing the word "theology," had said laughing:

"Ach ja, natürlich, Theologie: ja, ja, Theologie!"

And giving him a pat on the shoulder, sent him off.

Then, as he was returning to the bridge and the fear began to fade, he remembered me—he was reading a lot of Dostoyevsky and, besides, was a little in love with me—and that I was with those Italian SS, alone, abandoned, in the grip of terror.

Crossing the bridge he had seen me at the table and—he says—"as usual you were holding forth, with all those soldiers!"

He still reproaches me today for that bowl of bean soup as if it were Esau's mess of pottage. I could tell him that talking diminished my fear—that would please him, he knows that when I'm depressed I go out and talk. I talk to the baker, the butcher, the woman I encounter in front of a shopwindow, I give advice to the young salesgirl in the clothing store and with the porter I discuss politics.

But it wouldn't be exact; I was talking simply because it's pleasant to chat while eating bean soup; I don't remember if my "Italian SS" were very handsome like his German officer, I remember only the minestrone. Besides, I was sure he would come back. My optimism didn't ultimately lack a sense of reality, which at the time was linked to the moment and the unpredictable, and that morning it was confined within the circumscribed area of the big table and the pot under the gigantic horse chestnut. Or might it have been a plain chestnut tree?

Two weeks later, Giorgio was captured in Pinerolo as the result of a tip. I wasn't with him because I'd gone to Turin for an exam. I was, so to speak, in the literature department—I didn't attend more than five lectures, all in different places, because the university had been bombed—and I faced the difficulties of the trip (the Porta Nuova station was often bombed, and you risked having to walk for kilometers) only when there were exams.

I found out the same evening, and it was up to me to go to Pinerolo to search for him in all the barracks. That the racial flaw, remaining hidden in that declaration to the vice principal, could represent a risk didn't occur to anyone, least of all me. I was furious at him for stupidly getting arrested at the house where he always went (and brought me only once), facing dangers that were, naturally, pointless. Also, I was supposed to discover where they kept him prisoner by presenting myself—a ridiculous figure!—to the guard as his fiancée. I didn't find him: he had already been transferred to Turin and from there was deported to Germany.

I wrote him a letter in prison; it ended with the words "... in spite of all that"—the tour of the barracks in Pinerolo, which I blamed him for—"I love you."

My letter was written on very thin, durable paper. He brought it to Germany, and smoked it all there—he had learned to roll cigarettes and still rolls them today—right up to the words "I love you." Then he smoked those, too.

Talking, laughing, crying, and eating as much as I could when the opportunity presented itself, writing letters and walking in boots, in love and unhappy, I passed the war years the way I did any others. Very seldom did events frighten or sadden me.

Once in Turin I was seized by panic. I was crossing the Corso Vittorio bridge when the air-raid warning began to sound and right afterward came the siren.

I didn't like going into shelters—I still remembered the terrible stories of the first bombings in Turin: we'd seen the red flashes in a very clear night sky behind the shaking windowpanes—and I always tried to stay outside until the last moment. Then, as I had that time, seeing someone run, I began running, too. Thus with the others I reached one of the shelters dug under Monte dei Cappuccini, while the thuds of the first bombs could be heard in the direction of Mirafiori. When I glimpsed the black hole of the shelter entrance I immediately tried to separate from the crowd so as not to have to go in. But the people pressing me on all sides lifted me off the ground and transported me inside, bathed in fear down to my boots.

I was generally a prudent girl, uninvolved and often cowardly. Prudence abandoned me only during sudden bursts of rage. While my pity was directed mainly toward people I felt were like me, the rage that invaded me was immediate, blind, and uncontrollable, a rage against the oppressor, whoever it might be, and I abruptly lost any sense of distance and priorities. Rage boiled inside me when, riding in a tram forced to take a detour, I passed the men hanged on Corso Vinzaglio; the violence was all the greater given how impotent I felt, provoked that time even more by the dirty posters dangling above the hanged men than by the sight of their waxy doll-like faces.

I was already well aware that my sudden attacks of anger had nothing to do with courage conscious of its goal; as soon as they cooled off I regretted their effects and wasn't proud of them, but I had trouble controlling myself.

For a fit of rage against the literature teacher who had made fun of my friend Evi, I was suspended in the last year of middle school: I was the first girl in the school ever to be suspended. And on a much more serious occasion I risked my life and the lives of others.

One of the fascist soldiers in Torre Pellice had been murdered, and the funeral was planned—with the population invited to participate—for three in the afternoon. Shortly before three, something occurred to me that I wanted to tell a friend who lived in the "new houses," that is, the Collegio teachers' houses. So I hurried to her house: the street was deserted and the windows all shuttered. On the way home, as I emerged from the "new houses," I saw at the end of the street, right next to the monument of Pastor Enrico Arnaud, the fascist's funeral procession, a meager band of men in uniform, carrying the coffin on their shoulders. I turned and ran back into the house, but, five minutes later, a loud banging of fists against the door announced the fascists' arrival. They led us out, my friend, her mother, and me, and a small dark man, gesturing, ordered us to honor the coffin of their fallen comrade with the fascist salute: "I saw you, you scum, you were running home so you wouldn't have to salute at the funeral. Scum, like all the other scum in this town."

In front of the fuming little fascist, the familiar anger began to flare up. I thought: "Never ever will I give your salute." Then I perceived the two women beside me, my friend and her very pale mother—I remember them as looking in fact green—who were raising their arms, trembling. That visible tremor immediately shamed me—I wasn't yet frightened—and I raised my arm in the last fascist salute of my life.

As soon as the fascists had gone off on the road to the cemetery, my companions—we stood there as if of stone, motionless in front of the house—began to insult me. That agitated me much more than the preceding scene, since I couldn't bear to be called "crazy."

On occasions when I somehow realized (or feared) that I was making a poor showing, whatever the circumstances, values were flattened in the background and I remained alone in the foreground, with my clumsy gestures and my graceless appearance; I remained to recover or to defend.

In the last winter of the war I worked in Turin, where Franchi had given me the job of helping the French refugees housed in the barracks of San Paolo (with the assistance of a clandestine center that functioned almost openly with the usual imprudence, to me horrendous, in a noble palazzo, maybe on Via Maria Vittoria). With the five hundred lire a month earned in this job, I supported myself in Turin, where I lived not because of the refugees and still less because of the center on Via Maria Vittoria, but for love of my "A."

During visits to the barracks—in that extremely cold winter I had chilblains even behind my knees, and every so often Franchi, provided with a fake beard and false papers, came with me—we had met a French couple, no longer young. Their three-month-old child, a gray, stunted little creature whom the mother couldn't nurse, couldn't digest cow's milk, and wasn't growing well. Once, while standing there listening to the woman speak, swallowing her words— she was a mountain woman, closed and dignified—about the child to whom she was giving the bottle, we saw her burst into tears. The tears ran down her face, but she couldn't dry them because in one hand she was holding the bottle and in the other the child. Franchi, with a gentle, delicate gesture, took the bottle and held it at the right level—he was the oldest in a very numerous family—so that the baby could go on sucking while the mother dried her eyes. Yet again his gesture surprised me: I found the child with her faintly acidic odor not very attractive. She died shortly afterward of pneumonia, despite the powdered milk that Franchi had managed to unearth. On his orders I was to bring to the funeral an enormous, unwieldy flower wreath. I was furious because I had to ride the tram with that grotesque concoction and take part in an incomprehensible Catholic funeral with the sobbing parents beside the pale-gray baby's tiny coffin.

When they left, they entrusted me with some money that had been collected for the upkeep of the grave. I let days pass and, in the end, negligently spent the money on myself. I never went to the cemetery, where—certainly appearing ridiculous—I would have had to look for the custodian in the immensity of graves (the child's had its number) to find out how to discharge that duty.

I wrote in my diary: ". . . they think I'm sensitive; it's not true, I simply have an infernal pride."

I was fifteen when, on June 10th,[20] I went out to the square to listen to Mussolini's speech; I was twenty when I saw the Germans leave Torre Pellice. What are usually called the best years of one's life are for me contained between those dates. The war and the partisan struggle were part of my days

---

20 On June 10, 1940, Mussolini declared war on France and England.

not unlike the smell of the winter air and the sound of barking dogs on dark November evenings.

And here I was, an adult, considered adult, as if the preceding events—what happened, in other words—had caused me to grow up more quickly. But might it have been, I wonder now, an artificial growing up? Similar to that of the young thugs of the periphery today. The death of your contemporaries, the death you see hanging on the gallows with a livid face, fallen forward, can give you the macabre optimism of centenarians, an illusory sense of power, as if you now had in hand your conclusions and there were nothing else to aspire to. And so freedom gives you those feelings, freedom gained but not known, inherited not from parents but from grandparents, property that many of us weren't capable of handling and so it remained under our parents' management.

We lived like the crown prince who grows gray-haired and fat while the ageless old sovereign continues to govern and execute. We flirted with the heads of the conspiracy and told them about when we defended the republic, when we, too, were rebels. But we liked cigars and vacations in Biarritz. So they left us to it, even if we tended to have too many children.

The following little episode that I wish to recount here is perhaps a small premonitory symptom of these conflicts and late reflections that the war and the resistance sowed in me.

In 1946, we were involved in an orgy of theater productions. We performed all and everything, some better, some worse, with improvised companies and few essential tools.

I liked directing as much as performing. And so I produced in Torre Pellice not *Hedda Gabler*, alas, but Steinbeck's *The Moon Is Down*.

At midnight, the show over, we went home, the actors still dressed in German uniforms, and as we marched through the now empty, dark town, in the grip of a melancholy and sacrilegious mood, we intoned at the top of our lungs a German war song, as if to prolong in the streets the play that had just ended. Still singing, we marched up to the barracks next to the elementary school. At the time the barracks was empty and the entrance open. We entered the courtyard and sat on the steps. Little by little we fell silent, looking at the moon. Only at that moment did I realize that the war was really over, but that we were called back to it as to our youth itself by that enemy song, which condemned us to regret lost loves and dead friends.

I find in my diary on the date of April 29th the note copied below.

Torre Pellice had just been liberated; the Germans had left in their trucks; some fascists were running behind the last truck, trying to grab on to the edges of the vehicle. When the partisans arrived on our street, my sister and Marisa had gone to meet them carrying in their arms the guns belonging to some of the fascist boys whom they had persuaded to hide in the cellars and who would then be handed over as prisoners.

As soon as the Germans left, the town poured out onto the streets and a few hours later the beats of the big drum could be heard in the park. People were dancing and singing.

No one paid any attention to a group of French people who came down the road from Villar singing "The Marseillaise" to invite us to take advantage of the occasion and immediately free ourselves, period, from Italian domination.

In the hours after the Germans' departure I had had for the first time a terrible fear. I was sure they would return to take revenge—wouldn't I have?—and, besides, standing at the intersection of our street with the main street was a high cart, of a singular shape that recalled a kepi, loaded with weapons. That cart had been left behind by the fascist soldiers who had occupied our house for the previous two days, plugged up the toilet, and listened nonstop to the radio. I had picked up my books in a blanket and brought them to the cellar, and had slept there very peacefully on a straw mattress. Now though, I was afraid that an isolated shot would hit the cart and blow up the whole house, along with all of us.

In fact the Germans returned, and that same isolated shot, from a mortar, I think, didn't strike the cart but, instead, at the entrance to the town, destroyed the first truck in the column, which was carrying the flamethrowers, pulverizing it. The next day, people pointed out pieces of brain left stuck to the pavement at the sides of the road.

Once the fear had passed, I was plunged into the same state of depression I used to feel on my return from hikes in the mountains. Yet again the adventure had passed beside me and I had been unable to seize it and enjoy it; no way could I share in the general joy, and the years that passed, that became history precisely in the final success—O good, who have conquered evil!—seemed to me yet again an immense, senseless mountain of corpses.

I went to the cemetery alone. Right in front of the entrance, I found the doctor and the undertaker next to some open coffins. Inside, rigid corpses in fascist uniforms.

Back at home I wrote in my diary:

"Torre—evening April 29, 1945.

"Tonight you sleep, there in the cemetery, in rough caskets, without flowers, without tears, Germans and boys of the Littorio. I saw you today, you whom I do not know, on your back in the casket, your face fouled with blood and dirt, mouth open as if to shout, and your hands lying limp beside your body, hands of a boy, defenseless. The tombs of the partisans were covered with flowers. On the streets of the town there are flags. Brothers, forgive this joy; brothers, forgive the smile of mammas and wives; brothers, forgive the dead partisans what remains of them on earth, you who leave nothing, alone in a foreign cemetery."

In the margin, dated July 3, 1945 (I had happened to see the first documentary on the concentration camps, tacked on to the showing of a film in Turin):

"Buchenwald concentration camp. Brothers, I'd like to have the 'right' to forgive you."

In the preceding years a single cry wounded me to the core, beyond the barrier of complicit pity and impotent rage: pierced me, though it was still dubious as a presentiment. A cry that I might not have cried, but that someone cried to me.

One night, the Germans hanged a fifteen-year-old boy—I think from the Veneto—between Evi's hotel and the public scale. They'd found him sleeping, exhausted, on the mountain with a Parabellum pistol beside him. Evi had heard the din around dawn, had got up and opened the window. In the fading darkness she had heard the boy call to his mother. When she told me, the next day, I suddenly started crying, but the tears that bathed my face came not from my books and fantasies or, even further back, from my by now petrified childhood; they flowed from my body, which was aware of itself for the first time, and in which I would have liked to hide and protect the unknown boy.

Precise details about my father's death reached us ten years later, through information my sister got in a chance meeting in the United States with a distant cousin who had survived.

My father and mother, by now separated forever, had lived apart in Riga, bound by a lengthy court case, because each claimed custody of the daughters. I had found unguarded in the sideboard in the living room the entire package containing the divorce decree; the copy was in German, and Grandmother certainly was ignorant of the contents. The injured party was, surprisingly, my father; on the list of charges that the parties addressed to each other was a lineup of lovers attributed to the wife (unknown names, among which, unfortunately, was the notorious Spaniard), the venereal disease that the defendant had contracted from the accuser, the black eye witnessed by the maid as proof of the beatings given by the *signore* to the *signora*, the illegitimate birth of a child of my father's.

I hadn't told my sister about the document; she had been questioned after me in the living room and had decisively contradicted me, and would surely accuse me of disloyalty: I was guilty anyway of having guessed and betrayed. But I was silent above all out of shame. Shame for the two parties who were my father and mother, so similar here to the defeated for whom I felt both disgust and pity.

And yet reading the decree didn't prevent me from feeling a more profound pity for my mother. Compassion for her, surprised in her careless lies, which must have served to bolster her pride. And that was, in fact, the only pity I felt for her as an old woman, sitting erect in her beautiful beige-and-pink dress, the brooch on her shoulder, attentive to the conversations that were going on, her response prompt, her memory perfect.

Her unhappiness hovered over me like a distant cloud, high but dark. She wrote us tender letters; she arrived loaded with gifts. In the war years she came from Bulgaria, where she was the director of an Italian cultural institute after an eventful flight from Latvia during the Soviet occupation. She traveled on troop trains and brought suitcases full of sugar, prosciutto, chocolate, and even eggs. But upon her arrival— anticipated and so longed for—she took refuge in her discontent and always seemed on the verge of being disappointed. Only occasionally, at random moments, did I hear the resonant bold note in her voice again. She stayed shut in her room for hours, she smoked a lot, read, in a tone of irritation answered Grandmother (who in fact had a certain respect for her), and was not at all affectionate with me or my sister.

Between her and me, others had functioned as a screen. First the governesses who had brought me up as a child, then Grandmother, and finally Sisi, who could still make her laugh sometimes.

Once, when I was around fifteen, she found me in tears on the bench in the garden and asked what was wrong. I'd gone out a little earlier in a new dress, and had seen in the derisory glances of some schoolmates I'd run into in the square confirmation that the hem was in fact too long— the dress had been chosen by my mother (it pleased her) because it resembled the one in Botticelli's *Primavera*. I didn't dare insist on getting it shortened, so I answered that I was unhappy because I was ugly.

I saw a timid sorrow cross her face, as of apology, and I realized that she was looking for some words of consolation. Finally she said, "No, of course you're not, you have such beautiful hair!"

One afternoon when I was sixteen I went to the hairdresser and had my braids cut off: they ended in curls so perfect that my classmates hinted that they were made with curlers. When I came home with short hair, my mother, as meek as that time in the living room with my father, observed only: "What a pity, with your beautiful hair!"

Sometimes, instead, she exploded in sudden destructive outbursts where she seemed to let out, as if liberated, repressed storms, in a violent, even coarse language, in one hand a Bible and in the other a firearm. Any time I talked back she was surprised, and retreated, wounded by my rage.

Our fights were very rare, however (I didn't dare confront her, kept distant by her unhappiness), and often were expressed in letters left for one another on the table. If I was late returning from a vacation—in general, she couldn't stand the fact that I went on vacation—she wrote me furious postcards reminding me of my duties. She didn't trust the speed at which I studied and nagged me about the deadline for my exams although I wasn't at all behind.

I find her mentioned twice in my diary: in a half page of recriminations on family life: "Even a cat loves its kittens, but she doesn't reproach them for the milk given." And on the other hand, briefly, at another point: "My mother is a dear woman."

Of our father she never spoke. Sometimes Grandmother told us about him.

An acquaintance had gone—she recounted—to our house, where he lived with his daughter, whom the German mother, a nurse, had left with him, so she could return to Germany with a racially pure passport. He had to scrape money together after a bankruptcy and was selling furniture and fittings; leading the buyer around the house, he had asked him—Grandmother reported—if he wanted, in addition, Irene, the daughter, who followed him everywhere, clutching (I saw it immediately) his dressing gown.

I thought of this image often; it was the only one that resurfaced from a past gone by and concluded, submerged now and awaiting a future restorer. When I was a mother, writing my first book, I dedicated it to Irene, who died with him, at the age of six.

It seems to me that nothing else binds me to him, except the memory of that death and the voice I never heard of the child Irene.

His death remained within my life like a hidden seed, and gradually, as I lived and aged, it grew in my memory, not unlike a longtime love: nourished in part by tenderness for the young bodies of my children, for their gestures and laughter, for the limbs, gestures, and laughter of their friends. In this originated—late, as is my habit—my adult pity, the way jasmine produces runners that root in the earth from which they came. The only roots I recognize as mine.

As a Woman

Among all my friends,
    for Lalla

Once I could remember the dates of battles, the numbers of men and horses, the names of my students from ten years earlier. I would review a battalion of veterans, identifying them one by one. Now I want to shake off the names the way a dog shakes off rain.

I'll be sitting down to fantasize: I'll sniff the odor of the evening wind that's turned pure and crystalline after blowing thousands of miles across the desert.

I want to die in Piazza San Marco, my head on my knees.

But death throes in the middle of a square is inconvenient and ostentatious; certainly someone would come along and get rid of me, taking me to the hospital, where I'd die within the sanitary confines of a bed behind a green screen.

I suspect there's something illicit about fantasizing on my own—at my age—a gratuitous fantasizing that yields nothing, neither a written page nor a hope of anything concrete. There is in such fantasizing a hint of impiety, the intention to replace an act of faith, which is an end in itself. May I at least be allowed to die like Fuffi, the Siamese cat who after a move took refuge in an old linen wardrobe and there prepared for death, sleeping amid piles of freshly laundered sheets. He no longer ate, no longer peed; he opened his foggy eyes meowing when his master came to get him for the daily injection that even cats get these days, but so it is, you have to give some satisfaction to those who survive you. His fur lost its shine and under it Fuffi got thinner, clearly intending to disappear completely and forever in the linen wardrobe. Finally, the plaque with name and date—on the wardrobe, of course—again, to please those who survive you.

There is still something transparently ordinary in my fantasy, contained in the dailiness of the images; I will end up visiting, in imagination, deserts and mountains on group tours. All in all, a low-cost, almost permissible fantasy, with the modesty of flowering balconies and linen closets.

On television I prefer to choose programs that excite neither emotion nor thought. If I give in to extraordinary occasions—whether film or ballet or concert or opera—I cry. And similarly I cry when I reread the same books and even the same pages—unsure if I'm reading or remembering—of prose, usually. Poetry seldom moves me, not even German poetry. But I start repeating to myself, in my usual mutilated version, lines of Leopardi and even of Petrarch. Perhaps the time is near when I will weep, saying: "Sweet and clear is the night and without wind." And I don't know if I'm weeping out of a melancholy envy or, rather, because, in the beauty of something so perfect that I will never be able to re-create it, I feel my farewell ever closer.

But my weeping is transparently ordinary, too, since I'm now digging up right on the surface the topsoil of the years that remain. It seems to me that I bring little to light, and my curiosity about myself—with the fictions of a woman laid aside, what's left is to discover myself in the hardened sediments that old age will grow out of—is therefore a slightly fearful curiosity: How is it possible that I truly desire nothing besides life for my children and the absence of suffering for me? At what point and in what way—and how is it that I never realized it—and by what vortex was the intensity of emotions sucked up?

In the months after my hysterectomy I dreamed that an enormous, very healthy white tooth fell out; this irritated and worried me, but in the dream I kept repeating: it doesn't matter, I'll have a false one put in!

So I continue to have faith in artifice, in exercises for polio victims, in the grammar of children: "Let's say you was the mamma and me the papa." If I weep over a masterpiece, maybe my melancholy envy is, in the end, envy for an unattainable artifice. Will I be able to call this envy emotion?

In the future I give shape to an immovable laziness in which I am submerged as if in the sea still warm from the summer heat, the sun a little lower on the horizon, the beach empty, the sea at Carrara, where Giorgio taught me to swim.

I try firmly to keep before me the days that are more than thirty years behind me.

I had joined Giorgio in Carrara, in his house in Fossola, in September. I got married the following year—I'd known Gianni for three months and we were looking for a house, only the difficulty of finding one had kept us from marrying immediately—and some years later Giorgio left for Argentina, where he, in turn, got married.

In the morning we'd buy focaccia, still hot, at a bakery in Fossola, and some white grapes—it would be our lunch—and took the tram that went to the marina, the same one that carried the marble workers, whom I saw sitting exhausted on the seats.

On the beach there was only us; it was a fine September and in the sun we picked grapes in the vineyard at the foot of Giorgio's vegetable garden.

So he taught me to swim; he never scolded and always praised me. The first two successful armstrokes were like a baptism into the life of the body, repeated every time I've swum since then. Even today, I return from the pool purged in limbs and spirit, even if I smell of chlorine.

After our swim we lay on the sand and Giorgio taught me bridge, which I never played again after that. We stuck the cards in the sand and talked really about nothing until the sun sinking over the sea sent us home.

It may be that precisely in artificiality—in the construction of our emotions—old age is perfected. When, as an adult, wizened redskin, I sit in a circle of young people and teach them—not on the basis of my experiences: my experience is only the collective experience, as it is for every medicine man—I feel a tranquility, a secure expansion in space, certainly different from when I was younger and unable to separate from self-consciousness.

Not even to young women do I recount personal stories, but happily present negative examples—of how I was awkward and embarrassed and naive—that conceal a little laugh: I made it, let's see what you can do. But as my grandmother pitied me, I pity young women and try not to weigh on them, try to hide the deceptions that await them. And yet I wonder: Mightn't it be the usual naivete, not innocence but estrangement, that drives me to tell stories to those who have already dissected and dissolved these tales?

One of my current fantasies of flight: I'm sitting alone on the beach in a bathing suit, right on the line of the waves, head hidden by a big straw hat, dark glasses on my nose. I'm facing the sea and far off on the horizon is the sailing ship *Bounty*. I'm reading. Around me I hear the prattle of the usual stories and I imagine that—bent over my book, chin hidden by the hand in a gesture that rises to cover the mouth, while I gaze slowly at the sea—I look like an English spinster. In fact I'm clean, I don't soak my underpants in the sink, I love the fire chief and the crown prince; thus I loosen and knot ties easy to tighten and disentangle, and I also recognize in their stories—theirs, the women's—the unassuming and rational lucidity of my fantasies.

Maybe there has always been an old woman in me.

I wasn't beautiful (an unmediated beauty) in a family of beautiful women: Grandmother, my mother, my sister, and today my daughter. Now when I look at myself in the mirror I find my wrinkles beautiful, but a moment later I've stopped thinking about it.

It doesn't matter to me whether my grandchildren resemble me; nor indeed did it ever matter to me whether my children resembled me. Nor am I at all like my parents, though randomly heterogeneous elements inherited from everyone were repeated in me: my mother's thin eyebrows, the sharp, clear gaze I remember in my father, even though his eyes were black like my sister's and mine are brown. I have my paternal grandmother's beautiful hair, my father's large long hands, my mother's beautiful complexion. But as a whole I feel contained within a featureless interior "I," and at times I seem to resemble only my sister, whom I am so unlike; but I, too, wrinkle my nose when I laugh and cry.

As a woman I had to be born from myself, I gave birth to myself along with my children. And yet I've always thought and had fantasies about—and desired—men. For me, even the opera, which is beyond attraction and in fact chills and repels intimacy, carried the ornate plumage of allure. I of course wanted to be a woman, but I didn't immediately feel that I was one. That featureless interior of mine was also sexless, there was an indecisiveness between my desire and the achievement. And so the happiest moment of my life, the triumphal confirmation that I was in fact a woman—and from here the conclusive choice of being one—was the moment when I felt my daughter separate from me, with a slight but sharp, painless cut, preceding (though to me it seemed simultaneous) the grip of the forceps, exactly as one detaches a fruit from the branch.

I'm still, to this day, a woman in her; I like walking behind her, anonymous, hiding in her beauty. She proceeds confidently through the greenhouse where she's looking for a vine to give as a present. She explains to the young gardener what she wants. She considers herself timid—my mother also considered herself timid—and "not very identified with her role."

I seldom connect the tall, beautiful blond woman with the child I brought into the world and breast-fed, maybe partly because she, too, has children.

Only when I suddenly hear her voice on the telephone, tender with the guttural sound of her *r*'s: "Dove," I say to her, "dovey. Little tiger!" as when she was a child.

During long weeks I spent in the hospital where she worked in another department as a pediatrician, I'd hear her approaching in the corridor: her footsteps, like her father's, are also the rapid, light gait of a person more nimble than his weight. When she walks her ankles creak faintly. "Shitty ankles (or shitty veins) you made me, Mamma." Her defects or what she considers defects she'll gladly trace back to me or my mistakes. She even accused me of having swaddled her as an infant, the way people did a hundred years ago. That's why she has a belly. Every so often I defend myself: "look how I put the Band-Aid on your umbilical hernia; look, the varicose veins come from the Jarres, too. The belly, too!" But I don't dare say that I've never had a belly.

I walk behind her in the greenhouse, unobserved. I glance with my usual kleptomaniac's gaze among the vases—there are so many, no one would notice if I carried one off—while she proceeds creaking and proud.

I think of my hortensias, which are so thin. Laura, my daughter, always has splendid ones. She germinates sweet potatoes with long curled shoots, and her geraniums flower two weeks before mine. Asked as a child what she wanted to be when she grew up, she answered: "A lady, like Mamma."

Instead she works, as I worked and my mother before me. Every so often in my cuckoo-like detachment I make a sudden movement: Haven't I loaded her shoulders with a burden too heavy?

She mentions the unknown recipient of the vine; I, meanwhile, consider the climbing roses lined up in long rows with their labels. I can never guess if those stories of hers—the young recipient of the vine is separated from his wife and has a terrace exposed to the investigations of the old ladies opposite—are messages or random communications. I suspect her of having an appointment with a part of me I would prefer not to identify. Might it be "our bizarre superego" that she alludes to every so often? Damned, having escaped the snares of a rather wild upbringing, now it runs around on its own and passes itself off as me. I'm very slow in picking up the thread of my daughter's conversations, following an inner path that doesn't correspond to mine. I'm often surprised by the men she calls fascinating. Even the actors.

I decide on a yellow climbing rose. There was a yellow climbing rose on the chicken coop in Torre Pellice. Or was it white, one of those that flower right away and reveal a brownish-yellow heart when they open, as if they had been dipped in tea?

She tells me about the child. I find that she reasons with him too much, but I choose to be silent, just as I am while considering yet another rearrangement of the furniture, even though the wardrobe really doesn't go in the entrance hall. I'm slyly silent, and I relax. My gestures are manifested in her while she germinates potatoes and geraniums. Born whole and perfect not from my uterus but from my mind. Armed not by me, luckily, and not with my weapons: our kinship lies in my desires, satisfied yet so rarefied in my conscience that it's difficult for me to reawaken them. If I see her living and acting, she fulfills those desires expelled by my adult resolve. Always with some anxiety: she's not only unpredictable to me but, while I may fear for the safety of her brothers—I hug them and kiss them as if they were still my small children—I'm afraid of losing my intimacy with her, although it's uncertain and rarely spoken of.

What was I like as a young woman?

I got married in December of 1949. I had met Gianni in June of the previous year, and after two weeks we decided to get married. What decided me so swiftly—in the past I had always hesitated when someone proposed marriage, and I had never even thought of marrying my so madly beloved "A."—was a thunderbolt not so much of love, or not only of love, as of security. He was broad, blond, freckled, no taller than I was—as he ages he becomes gray over a reddish tint that wasn't noticeable before—though I had always liked tall, thin, dark men, and had kept photos of Gregory Peck on the wall. But he gave off a dazzling persuasiveness in which his passion for me merged with his brilliant intelligence. I yielded to this persuasiveness as to an adventure that would bring me the enchantment of the first real experience: love didn't return to me and wasn't even a conquest, but came from the outside, imposed itself like a "worldly" choice. I chose exactly the man whom the future suggested that I choose. I made a marriage of convenience in which the convenience had to do not with money, which I was indifferent to—we were dirt-poor—but with the superiority of the man who wanted to marry me.

I was very happy in the first years of marriage. Of the happiness I felt when I ran down across the lawn in Torre Pellice I can reconstruct the sensation that everything unpleasant fell away from me, peeling off; it wasn't yet happiness and was happiness no longer, while I was possessed by the certainty "I can."

Saying "I can," I let go of the tension of defense. As for the rest, happiness should be recounted as in a sequence of TV ads; it is in fact completely without irony.

At thirty-four, after ten years of marriage, I was expecting my fourth child. It wasn't a planned child, but I was very pleased because I liked having children and didn't think I'd have others; my third was three and a half.

My husband and I had spent Christmas vacation with the children in Val di Susa in a house we'd rented for the whole year; during that vacation it had seemed to us we were setting out toward a physical understanding that had till then been lacking in our union. It was a lack I didn't resent (that happened later, when it acquired the meaning of an object desired and not possessed), occupied as I was with having children, nursing them, moving—from apartment to apartment, each one lighter and bigger and nicer, like my mother's houses during my childhood—so it seemed to me that I had exactly what I wanted. Around me everything had the luminous clarity in which every question has an answer.

Of our Christmas vacation I remember the almost complementary joys of love at night and skiing during the day, when I felt I was slowly gaining confidence in my legs and my back, going up and down the small fields behind the house.

In general the fact that we had little money also contributed to my happiness, that we had to run up debts and then save to pay them, that we organized our life with little money. I kept the account book carefully, day by day. I was teaching outside Turin, in Settimo, and I traveled back and forth by train or bus. We didn't have a car: we bought our first one nine years after we married. I remember the happiness of my cold feet, in winter, as I looked out the windows of the bus at the plain stretching past Turin to Milan, furrowed by the black dots of the pylons. I can repeat only the word happiness, even though there's nothing particularly happy about the details that come to mind.

I greeted the certainty of my fourth pregnancy like a queen her crown. I didn't think of it as a risk to that timid start of sexual harmony between Gianni and me; rather, it was the demonstration of our new partnership, the child of love.

In reality I continued to be ignorant and alienated regarding the practice of sex; my husband contributed to this, and, not much more expert than I was, had, with a certain ill will toward the hostile female body, fueled my sense of guilt for my coldness. To the embarrassments of our generation, add our mutual insecurity, his reserve and my pride. He would never have talked about it, any attempt of mine shattered against his muteness. So—without realizing it—I got used to compensating for that failure of ours with the other riches of my life.

I had a blue skirt made; at the market I bought a piece of matching fabric and the usual dressmaker transformed it into the usual loose tunic. I was an elegant pregnant woman—I also had some beautiful blue-and-white shoes—even if my belly was a little larger than it had been the other times. The elastic stockings I had to wear weren't nearly as ugly as the thick, conspicuous ones I'd had to wear nine years earlier when I was expecting my daughter. My breasts were swollen and firm and paid no heed to the "you're irresponsible" of my friends and the silence of my mother; it seemed to me that my big belly radiated a beneficent aura that would heal everyone.

Never as in that spring had I been so available and understanding. I carried around my radiant belly and, protected by its halo, settled conflicts, found the right word or the suitable gesture to soothe and distract. Even my jealousy—Gianni often went out alone at night, I was too tired to go with him—fit with new urges in the physical union we'd hoped for and initiated.

And yet gradually I noticed that there was an impediment, an obstruction between him and me. He appeared listless and inert, scarcely livelier at the moment of goodbye, when he could go out. I was used to his silence—he who was so talkative away from home—and didn't feel it as a lack of response. I talked to him about everything, I told him everything. When we were separated, I wrote him long letters. Until then my talking and his silence had—at least so it seemed to me—perfectly complemented each other. And similarly my having children and his accepting them.

Naturally I tried to take him by the hand, to draw him out of a dimension that for the first time was secret. I needed him within the framework of my joy. But there was nothing to be done; he followed me passively as if merely giving in to the pressure of my hand.

The baby began to move, my face was round and rosy, and my three children put their hands on my belly to feel it rise and fall.

"That's the head!"

"That's the bottom!"

"No, it's a foot. Does he kick even when you go to the bathroom?"

When school was over, I bought a blue-and-green striped bathrobe that really looked good on me.

Sitting in the tram, in a June dusk, I looked out the window and, seeing the roofline of the San Giovanni Vecchio hospital against the sky, said to myself: "Someday I'll have to write about the roofs of Turin, in summer, when the swallows have arrived. They're very different. What are they like? Well, naturally, they're happy roofs."

I was finishing typing the manuscript of my first book, *Il tramviere impazzito (The Mad Tram Driver)*, and I was packing the suitcases to go to the mountains. I left the closets in the usual meticulous order: resoled shoes, attached to every child's coat a little bag with its scraps of fabric, the list of purchases to make in the fall. In the drawer of the small desk—which held the sheets of graph paper with the diagrams of the growth of my three children while they were breast-feeding—notes with the dates of vaccinations. In my suitcase the account book in which in September I would record, as I had for the others, the date of birth and sex of the baby. If it was a girl its name would be Anna.

As we did every summer, we were going to the mountains. I would be alone with the children for two weeks. The Venetian girl who had worked for us for six years had married; she would come later in the summer to help me and had agreed to return part-time in the fall. My mother would join us as usual around mid-July.

The house where for several years we rented a large apartment, which had no heat or hot water and whose kitchen had a cement floor, was very cheap. In winter we lighted a big woodstove and in front of it at night I bathed the children in a tub. It was an isolated house, adjacent to ruins and empty cottages. By day full of sun, by night dark. Years later, my children confessed to me that the perpetually broken streetlamp in front of the house had been used by them for target practice.

Through a door in our bedroom there was access to vast, empty attics above uninhabited apartments. The door had never been locked: that sort of carelessness was typical of the house and we were used to it. As we were used to the faint illumination of dim lamps that hung in the most unexpected places.

My husband hurriedly deposited my pregnant body and my children and left: I felt a relief in him as he set out toward cool evenings on the Po with friends, unmarried men and sterile women.

The first night I couldn't sleep: the floor of the attic creaked as if someone were walking there. It creaked all week and I kept waking up.

The following Sunday I told Gianni, who had come in a hurry to get clean shirts:

"Listen, the door to the attics doesn't lock."

"Tell Galli," he said.

That Galli was our imaginative landlord. He provided us with what he felt like: excellent salad, rather dirty blankets, a large, clean, fenced courtyard, and the many dim lamps that lighted odd corners.

Neither Gianni nor I liked practical matters and bureaucratic ones even less—I out of timidity, he out of laziness (he was never timid)—and we tried to unload those tasks on each other. He was exceptional on exceptional occasions: he slept on the floor next to the bed of a child who'd had an operation; he brought another to the children's hospital to have a cut sewed up. He gave injections with a light, steady hand. He walked on the roof like a cat to straighten a fallen chimney. He also went to two funerals in one day, while I stayed home.

In daily life—apart from sporadic attacks of guilt, as a result of which, in an effort to score points, he washed the dishes—he was in general absent and resentful: I had gotten him into that mess and now he was the one who had to kick the children crawling over his feet while he was on the telephone; yet he never took the initiative to have the phone moved from the hall to the living room. He was extremely disorganized—owing to a primordial disorder—but, once a year, amid clouds of smoke, in an atmosphere of imminent disaster, he prepared the tax returns, with such meticulous care that the tax consultant whom he had to turn to in the end, said, looking at our documents, that she had never seen more masochistic returns.

Only after nineteen years did he allow me to become a signatory on our meager bank account; I don't think it was out of distrust—it simply hadn't occurred to him before. Similarly, we were the last in Turin to have our bills paid by bank transfer.

So of necessity I found myself on the front lines of the daily routine. I didn't grieve over it as an injustice; I respected my husband's scientific work—I also admired it—and it seemed to me that I personally had to respond because he had to hustle so hard for us. I wasn't yet making comparisons between him and me; gigantic energies overflowed from my happiness.

Naturally I didn't talk to Galli about the door. I was afraid of making a bad impression: the floor creaked night after night, always in the same way, and nobody appeared. Inside me the baby moved—he was already a child who didn't sleep at night—and when I got up to listen at the door of the room opposite, I heard my children breathing peacefully in their sleep.

I went back to bed and lay down, hands crossed over my belly. I was awake and I thought: confused and impotent thoughts, scraps of thoughts that whirled mostly around the nearly eleven years of my marriage and what there had been in those years between Gianni and me. But I was afraid to face the facts, to extract them from that aura of happiness in which I had immersed them up to then, to examine them, evaluate them with the cold gaze of my adolescence. I isolated some individual events and pondered them, and then, when I should have connected and dissected them— or even gone back to the times that preceded Gianni's and my meeting—I quickly pushed them away. Even my jealousy—in Turin, my husband preferred to go out with a woman friend of ours—was, like my thoughts, confused and impotent.

Sometimes I re-created the old willow that had been uprooted right next to the garden fence: twisted and bare, near sunset it turned all to gold. Here and there a few branches still grew out of the trunk, yet as the sun went down you couldn't turn away from its light. When I arrived that year, it had just been pulled out of the ground. I had always said to myself that I would like to write about it and the black crow that would wait for the gilded moment to sit right in the middle of the cavity at the top of the bare trunk and sing. Now it seemed to me that I could no longer describe it, as if the opportunity had escaped me forever.

I was there, crushed in that uncomfortable double bed in which seven months earlier we had conceived our baby, and I couldn't move, I couldn't do anything. I wasn't me at all, I was only my belly.

The Saturday before, while Gianni was putting shirts and underwear in his bag, I had said to him:

"Why don't you come a little earlier next week, instead of getting picked up by the police?"

It was the summer of 1960, and he had excitedly told me how he had dodged the armored police cars, jumping from column to column along the arcades of Via Po.

"You don't understand," he had said, "it makes me feel like I'm still young."

I was what kept him from that, me with my belly.

And another time, when, at the last minute, as usual, he was working night and day to finish a job, he had reproached me because I protested:

"You don't understand, I'm in a battle with time!"

I was she who didn't understand, she of the suitcases, the measles, the whooping cough, she who was always tired and had a stomachache. She of the bad moods: he came home— as late as possible—and there I was, tired and in a bad mood. The children, however, washed, fed, and already in bed.

When had I ever been happy? I was depressed as a rule. Terrified before every birth. With each child, in fact, I was more afraid.

Slowly, wakeful night after night, as I listened to the old attic creak, knowing that outside was the terrible moonlit night of the mountains, so narrow and black in the valleys and light and airy on the peaks, my joy ran out like blood from a body fatally wounded.

"I'm an unmarried mother," I said one night in a sudden flash of rational illumination, one of those flashes that go on burning in me, feeble but necessary, in a small luminous circle, like a candle on the table. "I've always been an unmarried mother."

The baby moved violently, aimed to the right and then exploded in a series of softer little kicks, communicative. I seemed to be shut up inside my belly with him.

A month later that same summer, I wrote a long letter to my husband, who was camping on Elba with our two oldest children. I asked him to answer. In our shared life I wrote only one other letter on that subject, the two of us, that is, and what would become of us. Neither the first nor the second ever received an answer. The second I later found among his papers, and, as I did with the letters written to my mother, I took it and kept it.

As for the first, he told me once that he had lost it on Elba, in a café while "he was thinking what to answer."

In fact he couldn't answer, and that impossibility, which clashed with my eternal need for clarity (here, truly, he Catholic and prudent and I Protestant and imprudent), started the long evolution that led to the end of our marriage—though not of our understanding—without, however, lowering his defenses so far as to put his equilibrium at risk: this I didn't even hypothesize, I had so firmly constructed it along with our union, walled it into the foundations of my personal happiness.

One night three weeks before the baby was born, I dreamed that I was with my three children in an airport in a broad desert valley. With others we were waiting for the end of the world. The valley was rimmed by low morainal mountains, and the sky above their straight flat line was illuminated by a pale and violent inner light, which announced that disastrous event and turned the stone of the valley gray. When it came—and I don't know how to describe it except as a stellar wind—I threw myself on my children. We survived and, when the catastrophe passed, I got up again. My children were unharmed, except for the youngest, who had a tiny bleeding wound in the corner of his mouth. I woke in the night with a start, and felt the contractions slowly beginning and only toward morning stopping.

The child who was born in September was a beautiful boy—I called him Andrea—with dark eyes and hair, a round, pale, solid face. When I attached him to my breast, he grunted, sweet and determined as a young wolf.

I never felt him as I did the three others. He was, yes, my child, and the same ties bound me to him, but he was also another, come from who knows where, out of I don't know what desire, maybe on that stellar wind.

My attachment to him who so sweetly grunted while he suckled was, unlike my attachment to the other children, besieged by fears, as if at any moment I would lose my grip, and my capability as a mother would vanish. That child, though so healthy and strong and handsome, might disappear just as he had appeared. Even now that he's a man, I'm always afraid when he's far away that he won't come back, that he won't phone, won't write, that he'll be silent forever. That he won't recognize me.

As he grew, I was bringing up his sister and two brothers with a few basic but fixed rules. And at school, too, I was bringing up children—I who so loved to stay in my corner was always in the midst of others—and it didn't much matter what I taught, the subject was the means, never the end. I tried to take away their fears; in fact, that may have been the only common element in raising children at home and at school. Here I shouted gladly: "I'm not your mother!"

Laura and Pietro (the "uneven" ones in birth order) say that basically only Paolo had a mamma. "Paolino," they warble, imitating what they say is my voice when I speak to him or about him. Paolo laughs and Andrea listens silently. Again his dark, nocturnal animal's silence intimidates me.

While I wanted the three others—a single whole, from which he lived apart—to obey those fundamental rules, with him I gave in, as if he carried his rules within himself. He got up from the table before we'd finished the meal, even if we were discussing something that concerned everyone. The others pointed it out to me. Laura recalled the day she had to eat the pasta she had rejected sitting on a stool in the bathroom, the plate on the toilet lid.

Andrea stayed awake at night reading. Once I went into the room, and he looked up from the book: *Purgatory*! "It's wonderful," he said without enthusiasm, making a statement.

Sometimes he told me his dreams, but he usually didn't confide anything else. The following dream he wrote to me because he didn't feel like telling it:

"There's knocking at the door. I open it and see first of all Grandmother in a big hat like a sombrero that makes her youthful (strange, after climbing the stairs she's not even out of breath), my sister, who is with her, and Aunt Sisi. I'm glad, it's the first time they've seen my house, and I want to be hospitable. I shift the chairs so they can sit down, but it's hard for me to move: the place is very small and I have to gauge my movements. As they start talking, I want to make tea: I climb up on the stool to get what I need, open the cupboard, and with great disappointment see that my mother, who meanwhile has appeared on the scene, has arranged her china where my kitchen things should be. I'm angry, I can't prepare anything anymore. My first instinct is to throw everything on the floor, but I restrain myself, and I hear my sister saying I'm right. My mother would like to make me accept the fait accompli, but, looking down at her, staring into her eyes, I grab the two most beautiful pieces of china and throw them on the floor, one after the other. My mother, unmoving, imperceptibly bites her lower lip, and I stop, because I understand that my gestures have now lost their dramatic power.

"We're downstairs, it's dinnertime. My mother, instead of giving me food, puts in my mouth a rough shard from one of the pieces of china I broke, saying to me bitterly: 'Look, it's the most valuable thing I have.' I insult her: 'Shithead, I have only four cubic meters and you want to take half.' My father intervenes, inopportune as always, saying that perhaps 'shit is a heavy word.' Instinctively I respond, 'Coward, then,' and immediately it occurs to me that that was the right term to wound her. Even if I'm overwhelmed, I cry and shout, I'm satisfied with my revenge. I wake up sitting on the bed, repeating, now without conviction: 'She's the one who *started it.*' "

When did I ever possess "china"?

That I might be so hateful and hated in my children's dreams doesn't worry me; I flow in countless streams within them and my mistakes as a mother belong to the mistakes contained in the lunar vessels of everyone's follies. Whatever they may have been, they will bear fruit, I tell myself, and I have no power over that fruit, whether sweet or bitter. They don't seem settled, fixed in themselves, defined.

I have only sporadic and fleeting feelings of guilt toward my children; but I still shiver sometimes and regret that I kicked Andrea out of the house when he was eighteen, putting two empty suitcases and a hundred thousand lire on his bed. His sudden absences, my not knowing where he was or with whom, put me in a state of such anxiety that I preferred to know that he was out of the house, on his own, so that I wouldn't have to wait every time, tormenting myself, for a sign of life from him.

I've always had constant, real feelings of guilt toward my books; the only real guilt is "not writing."

Nor did I have any guilt feelings toward my students. In a period when confessing collective mistakes had become fashionable—on the example of certain politicians who rightly should have blamed themselves for absolutely individual ones—one of my principals had said during a teachers' meeting, ". . . because we're all guilty!" At which I stood up and responded, "Not me."

Passion for my work, in fact, cleared me of second thoughts and doubts that were not technical corrections. When, standing in the doorway of the classroom, I looked for a moment at my students and saw them returning promptly from the tumult of recess to their places, where they rose with respect, I was the State, looking with severe eyes on the disorder that was to become order. I was happy to say, "I'm a service of the state, a service that works. Why don't you take advantage of me? There aren't many state services that do function."

I scolded them: "Damn Italians." I provoked them: "You won't get rid of me so easily." And day after day I went to school, even if I was coughing, had a runny nose, an aching back. I was the state, even with arthritis and bronchitis.

Naturally I also enjoyed being the state. I said: "You know what you make me think of, Giuseppe, when you have to use your mind? Of the big ape in the savannas who gets up on his back legs for the first time, looks at his hands"—I mime the gesture—"and asks himself: 'Huh, what's this?'"

Next time the class asks: "Will you do the big ape of the savannas again?" Giuseppe smiles, not at all offended, the scoundrel; he even seems pleased to be the center of attention. My little philistines are never offended. Once, one of them asks me: "When will I stop being a damn Italian?" They also reproach me—I'm very proud of their reproaches—and complain about me to me. Salvatore, a small Neapolitan with a strong nose, criticizes me one day for not correcting everyone's mistaken pronunciation of the French silent *r*. "Look," I apologize, "when someone makes a lot of mistakes I correct mainly the more serious ones first."

I don't know how much of me had been absorbed by the time I left them, after the final exams. I couldn't teach much; taught most of them to read correctly and understand what they read, a few to write. I once managed to get out of a gang leader the Calabrian (Latin and Arabic) terms for "cherry" and "stupid," and he had agreed to grant five minutes of attention to the blackboard on which I had written the Latin and the Arabic.

A victory no more solid and lasting than the one gained in three minutes during a recess when, in an almost complicit impulse of trust, the same boy confesses that he crucified a cat and skinned it alive: "I committed a murder." He's red and sweaty with the emotion of his revelation. I give up correcting him in order not to interrupt.

For those three minutes I suffered, acknowledging that at any moment they could be revoked: the gang leader would continue to write "Down with the Jews" on walls and, wearing a ski mask with eyeholes, maroon scarf around his neck, would wreck the market stalls near the stadium; and, similarly, the girl with humble eyes whom I had managed to get to pronounce precisely the personal pronoun *je*—I had a well-founded suspicion that the use and meaning of that "I" was as difficult as its pronunciation—and who though still thin from ages of hunger was already developing some curves from eating processed food (just enough to turn her into merchandise), would sell herself for a few lire.

I couldn't forgive those who bought them, even if for different purposes, with the few lire, with an ice cream, a pizza, a class trip provided by the money of well-to-do parents: Weren't they destroying that fleeting parity, entrusted to achievements not mine, which I had been able to reach in the corridor in those three minutes?

I felt a singular bitterness, and it was that of the enormous divide between the effort made and the result. It was in any case a bitterness common to those who, like me, great or small, had to support the Italian state in those years. Besides, although my career was disadvantaged and subordinate, it didn't seem like a waste to me. The satisfaction—in fact, the fulfillment—I got from exercising my damn little Italians, my little philistines, led me in the end to support the poorly developed and poorly regulated rite of careless bureaucratic performances, phony programs, meetings with an eye on the clock, words without reason that from minister to minister perpetuated impotence. Sitting in the back row in the teachers' meeting room, I read novels during assemblies—I reread all of Proust—and only every so often, raising my head from my book, allowed myself mocking comments on the ministerial newsletters.

Only with a few colleagues did I find a common understanding. When, for about a year, I'd had official responsibilities on the school board, I realized—to my surprise—that I had lived till then in an ideological isolation that, working in the classroom with students, I'd been completely unaware of. Now I stood before the enemy, with my meager, ingenuous, and partisan tools. To find a solution for even a tiny problem (I discovered I had a different concept of priorities), I would have to embark on a slow, careful political scheme. I lacked a suitable language, I was direct and sometimes deliberately inappropriate; at home, the children made fun of me: "*Barbetta*"—or even "Mittel-European"; that is, Protestant—"here's the same old *barbetta*." My obstinacies had for them something exotic in which they couldn't distinguish the Lutheran devil (certainly not Mittel-European) from the *barbetto* God, who continued to insist that any battle was worth the fight provided it was a good one.

But I faced yet more proof that institutions rejected me. My snobbishness as a member of a minority by now gave me only scant satisfaction, and I stubbornly persisted in useless, exhausting efforts that sank in the Catholic swamp.

I was fifty, and I got up at six thirty in the morning to take the tram—my school was on the outskirts—in the cold, still Turinese winter mornings. At the end of the day I was aching with exhaustion all over. But I didn't feel like giving up either teaching or the work at home; casual conversations with colleagues, the hours in class, the piles of laundry to iron, all anchored my days. School on one side, home on the other, they were the mutual alibis by which I didn't have to be completely available to anyone. They were obliging grooves that nevertheless gave me the only possible freedom, that of a certain mental reserve.

In my big, increasingly empty house—Laura and Paolo now lived on their own and I had premonitions of the departure of the other two—I had become used to doing all the work myself and I went through the rooms in silence, no longer followed by the complaints of those women who worked for me part-time. Sometimes for days I'd leave dust on furniture previously polished with great care. I avoided seeing people who had been our friends as a couple; every so often I'd march, slightly out of breath, in a demonstration in which I could shout my rage aloud, and only in an occasional resurgence of activism did I prepare one of those great dinners I'd enjoyed cooking for the whole circle of our friends.

Only writing took me out of the darkness. Writing was within the narrow measure of my mental reserve. Erasing my tracks as usual, like an Indian being followed, I wrote *La Principessa della luna vecchia (The Princess of the Old Moon)*, the most cheerful and ironic of my books, dedicated to my children and their friends, the only future that seemed possible.

There was a separation between Gianni and me that lasted years. Our life as a couple seemed over; having won a room for myself, I closed the door at night after dinner and didn't respond even to the ringing phone. Gianni didn't speak to anyone and didn't speak to me; at the table, alone with me, he didn't ask for the salt or the wine, he pointed.

I was going through a difficult menopause that I tried to control by means of hygienic and psychological rituals. I certainly wasn't capable of evaluating the scope of my troubles: I was used to the idea that my imagination exaggerated them. I got my revenge even on the malevolent rule of the Fathers stating that one must suffer in silence; I treated my body that—I kept saying to myself—was no longer pleasing to a man or a newborn, and that had always been alien to me anyway, like a machine I had to maintain so that it would function. I was terrified that it would disobey, and I watched it from up close: cut out the rusty gears immediately, get rid of the broken parts, prostheses, hooks, switches.

I'd had a turtle for a few months. I had managed to get it through the winter in a hole dug in the soil inside a chest on the balcony. In spring I had fed it a salad it was very greedy for. I got up early even when I didn't have to go to school—I often slept badly—and first of all went out to the balcony and called it. Hearing my voice, it moved its legs and pushed its head out of the shell.

One May morning I was awakened at dawn by a storm. I went to get Lipitza—we had found it in Yugoslavia as it was crossing the street—and placed it on the floor at my feet with its ration of salad. I was correcting homework; outside, the black-and-white dawn was striped with lightning flashes. Lipitza, having eaten the salad, lay down, legs extended and head resting on my shoe. My only gestures of tenderness were for its fetal acts.

Resentments proliferated in my mind. I couldn't forgive our mutual friends (my ex-friends, I called them to myself) for not perceiving the distance—measured not by events, however, but by inflexible, intimate conclusions—between my appearance and my frenzied inner world.

I didn't dare to separate from Gianni even though no day passed when I didn't think of it. I was restrained by the nagging thought of what both he—whom I was used to caring for—and, above all, my children would do. I couldn't impose on them what had been imposed on me. To let my image as an optimistic and tenacious mother fade. But more than anything else I held on to a firm idea of the unity of our nuclear family, and it seemed to me that I intuited in its cohesion a secret force that was stronger by far than my personal possibilities. When my daughter, at the age of twenty, left us with a sudden, violent act of revolt, amid my cries of despair, anger, and surprise, I felt that her departure made a burning wound in the heart of this nucleus, as if by leaving she had also carried off a living part of her brothers.

My resentments became furious when, during evenings with friends, I heard Gianni speaking, charming and inventive—yet again I unlikable, the other appealing, he the artist, I the drone—and I recognized his juggler's tricks. As a faithful old partner, I couldn't reveal them, an ally in spite of everything. The struggle grew by the hour; the awareness, even here, of my isolation, and of the impossibility of breaking it by persuading others, sometimes led me to wild explosions of protest. Shouting on behalf of the oppressed—my bursts of anger were usually on political subjects—I was shouting on behalf of myself.

I was sitting, mortally weary, like a corpse in which a support stick has been inserted between back and overcoat, and I looked at my ex-friends, his accomplices. Had even one of them urged me to be "good" with him who was so good, "the poor fellow"? Of course I, too, was afraid of appearing mean to the children if I abandoned their father, helpless, in the woods.

In the meantime, my mother, who was now seventy-nine, had on the advice of her doctor—she had fallen and fractured two vertebrae—and at my insistence moved to our house. I needed to simplify the problem of how to help her, I felt responsible for her, and I thought that if she lived with us it would be a matter of providing for her, so independent and lucid, that bit of nursing and domestic help that I was used to giving all my family.

When, twenty-six years earlier, I had told her I was getting married—unexpected news, because what sort of man (or here, too, "the poor fellow") "would be so crazy as to marry you!"—she had had a beautiful trousseau made for me and had given me the most valuable piece of furniture she had, a nineteenth-century cherrywood writing desk.

She could barely forgive my sister for her divorce from a man who seemed exceptional and never asked her the reasons. No one could have been worse than the husband from whom she herself had had to separate. When, years later, I explained the reasons for my sister's divorce, she appeared surprised (and incredulous) and changed the subject.

Once I was settled in my marriage, she periodically gave me beautiful and useful presents for the house. She kept any possible confidences at a distance with both arms; my condition as a "happily" married woman governed and limited our relationship. Naturally she favored my husband, and she came to me through my children, whom she loved without preference or distinction, showering them with presents and following their adventures.

A photograph of her: she's sitting erect on the beach, a pale skirt under a pale sweater flaps in an almost autumnal whiteness; around her Laura, Paolo, and Pietro, as children. She smiles with a happy, rapt smile, not at the photographer but at the September day.

I continued to court her, to challenge her to the intimacy that would have confirmed her affection, and sometimes I seemed to pirouette around her to win her approval. Every so often I had fits of rage and hatred—and then one of those very rare fights broke out—because she never failed to keep reminding me of any help she gave. I tried to turn to her as infrequently as possible, because I couldn't bear those complaints.

Not at all obsessive about money, which she still earned, working—I was never afraid of being without it—generous and magnificent in her gifts, she was capable of reminding me years later that she had once had to wipe the bottom of one of my children, and if for some reason I had no household help, it seemed that I demanded that she wash the dishes. Between her and me, between her generation and mine, a real class difference widened; she wasn't used to manual labor (which if necessary she did extremely well)—she had had baby nurses, governesses, cook and maid, and thus had never considered the amount of work I'd had to take on.

We also had moments of serenity, talking about my children, books, her translations; she translated from Russian, she was modest, exacting, grateful for the beauty of the text she was translating, fierce about others' mistakes.

In summer, after a month spent together (not without storms, because, naturally, she wasn't used to staying with others, and the grandchildren, taken all together, were a little less adorable), she lived by herself in our house in the mountains, watered the flowers, polished the doorknobs, read her books in the sun; when she returned to Turin in September she was tanned and wrinkled like an old Angrognina.

In the city she came to us every night at quarter to seven from her small bright, elegant apartment, near ours. She talked to the grandchildren, who were having a bath and getting ready for dinner. She smoked in every corner of the house—she didn't stop smoking until the age of eighty, and I dared to make fun of her, saying "virtue takes the slow road!"—and once she crushed a lighted butt in a fried egg, mistaking it for an ashtray (she was very nearsighted). When she was making something to eat, one of the grandchildren observed the cylinder of ash as it got longer and longer, balanced over what she was cooking. Meanwhile she would talk about her job—she taught French in a middle school—and her sharp, well-honed insults, especially about her principal, were probably the first swear words my children heard from the mouth of an adult.

Alone with me she was cautious and slightly ill at ease. One afternoon when she was already old she summoned me to her house, and, reminding me of "everything she had done for my children," charged me to hand over, after her death, her most valuable objects, the ones she cared about most, to my sister, who didn't have children and who, after her divorce from her American husband, lived and worked in Turin. Pressing together her lips, which she dampened a little with her tongue, she spoke with precision: the Russian silver, Grandmother's worktable, the prints, and two eighteenth-century porcelain vases. She scrutinized the room with her small, light brown eyes, as if to forget nothing. I had so profound a fear of her closed face that, witnessing her as she lay dying, I winced if an unconscious shadow of severity ever crossed it.

So as she searched with her gaze, it didn't occur to her—in her mind I had been so subsumed by my children—to leave to me any object she cared about.

From my grandmother's house I kept the big pale-walnut Provençal wardrobe, the small painting of her parents' house, the little table that held the Bible in the living room, a small chair, and Grandfather's Bible, in which someone had stuck a scrap of paper, the writing on it already unsteady, noting Mark 4:35: "... *et Jésus dit: passons à l'autre rive.*"[21] Grandfather's books.

And two large porcelain cups, with pink painted roses, one without a handle; I use it in the morning for breakfast.

Returning home after that monologue of bequests, I was distressed and disturbed. It seemed to me—and I was childishly resentful and uneasy—that the old blackmail leaked out of my mother's words: "When I'm not here anymore, you'll see." But that list especially upset me, it was so precise, delivered with compressed lips and evasive eyes. The bequests didn't matter—it was true, besides, that my mother had lavished gifts on her grandchildren, had bought games, books, clothes, taken them to the movies, the circus, the beach— and yet I felt (and was wounded by it) that, as usual without appearing to, she had intended to exclude me from her silver, from her eighteenth-century vases, from her prints, and gradually from the drawers with the powder-colored nightgowns, cream-colored gloves, the gold pin with the cameo. From the secret of her preciousness. Maybe, I tried to convince myself, she wanted to trust me, by making that consignment, but I swallowed my tears and wondered: I would never succeed in understanding her.

Behind her unease and my fear, we both remained stuck at the same point where we'd left each other in Riga. Each of us probed what was dissimilar in the other: I, in her, her reluctance. Absolute in her passions, she either loved or hated; unable to mediate, she would suddenly cast off those

---

21 "... and Jesus said, 'Let us go over to the other side.'"

she considered unworthy or unfaithful, with the same secret joy with which she annihilated me in her furious judgments, but she called on reason as a motive for her abandonment. She, in me, my need to convince and conquer, thus my indiscretion. I wouldn't easily resign myself to losing someone, I calculated, but my reasonableness led me to find a justification for everyone. Behind a deliberately shut door, she might not give in for years; I was always ready to turn back at the first blandishment. If I barred the door—I, too, was very touchy—I stayed close to it hoping to be called back, and consoled myself by fantasizing. She hated fantasies and was ill-suited to imagination (translating Pasternak in masterly fashion, she constantly asked me for confirmation: "Do you think it's possible that this is really what he wanted to say?"), so she detested my fantasies and saw my imagination as a lie.

After her death, I had to put her things in order and found some letters that were still sealed. Letters from some aristocratic German women with *von* surnames—*"Liebes Signorchen . . . "*—had never been opened, including even the last ones from Tante Erna, dear friend and aunt of our childhood. In Germany my mother also corresponded with the former head of her office in the economic section of the German command in Turin, where she'd worked as an interpreter. She, who regularly passed on information to the resistance movement, admired that pacific and honest man, who after the war wrote to her at length: *"Liebe, sehr verehrte Frau Coïsson . . . "*

The letters from the cousin who had sent the news of our father's death were unopened, apart from the first, closely written on sheets of transparent paper. My mother had never let us read it, although she reported to us the contents. The cousin had written again, asking why she hadn't had a response. Also unopened was a letter from my uncle's lawyer, in which he insisted on clarifying the situation of the house in Torre Pellice following a lawsuit with a negative outcome for my mother.

She had never opened that correspondence—as she hadn't left any written note of her wishes—but had kept it intact in her drawers, delivering herself, hidden, to me.

In reality we were present to each other in the first person, above all and only, in the letters we exchanged, a probably decisive epiphany on many occasions.

As soon as she settled in with us, with her furniture and her things, in her tidy, polished room—she hired and paid a woman to come three times a week to clean it, and the other rooms as well—an implacable light was shed on my shadows, tracking me down in the most silent moments, the most remote corners. If I was concealed there with an image of my children's childhood, an inexact family date, some buffoonery, there she was, precise, cutting me out in a dazzling blade of light, reducing, diminishing, dispossessing.

In my limbo I took shelter in a hazy existence, with no outlines: I wandered back and forth on the pathway of the same thoughts—whether to end my marriage, stay alone with the two children who were still home, find a small house near the school—and tried to gather, here and there, in a disordered, slightly maniacal way, the crumbs that were exclusively mine to keep. In my mind I made lists of what I still cared about and what I would throw away without regret. I had emptied my room of furniture, placed my books, my necklaces, lotions, and some unframed photographs on metal shelves inherited from a child's room.

I tried to get rid of the womanly ornaments that remained to me. I have no further need for symbols, I said to myself: the cup with blue-and-white squares (the only relic of my childhood in Riga), my newborn daughter's pink undershirts, the silver vase dented because it frequently fell off the small dresser in the entrance hall, knocked down by the children hurrying by.

One night I threw my wedding ring in the toilet.

I treasured, on the other hand, even casual encounters, with anyone.

With the beautiful unknown woman I met in Piazza San Carlo during a demonstration one morning in June, 1976. I wandered here and there in the crowd of young men and women, in blue jeans or flowered skirts, clogs on their feet, children astride shoulders, young policemen in civilian clothes with faces freshly shaven amid those slightly dirty youths with their red flags. I was obviously the only mother in the square—the only father, Vittorio Foa, was on the stage—and I couldn't make up my mind to stay. Until, behind the stage, I found that other mother of my age, in a tight flowered dress, also in search of a place. We talked for a few minutes, she gazed at me with beautiful luminous green eyes. She had eight children—she told me (her dark hair was streaked with white)—and she had left home with the younger ones. She was on their side, against her husband and the older children. She spoke calmly and decisively.

I often took long walks on the streets on the hill, alone, or sometimes with my friend Lalla. We sympathized with each other over our vertebrae—her neck hurt, as did my back—which at a distance of centuries still felt the dampness suffered by our common forebears (she on her father's side, me on my mother's) while they defended the faith up in the mountains.

In our peaceful words—I told her the names of trees and flowers, we talked about school and books—common sense prevailed, having descended along with arthritis from ancestral caves. A bitter choice that strains to straighten the back and that, in truth—we both knew—offers few consolations, besides trust in our companions who share this reasoning. A simple and modest occupation, suited to the steps of those climbing up and down.

At home, when I was driven out of my corners, my possible dissatisfactions could be due only to my bad character. Of the terrible inner fury that without direction or purpose gnawed at me, my mother, innocent and indifferent, absorbed by her own complaints, perceived nothing and continued to lay her troubles on my "happiness," as she called it.

Precisely defined and returned to my role as a bad girl, I struggled within the maternal constraint that seemed to repeat and emphasize the wrongs I'd endured in my life as a woman: the disavowal of the necessary work of my hands, taken for granted, the solitary burden of responsibilities, also obvious.

I had leaped over an untasted maturity not into the resignation of old age but into the disorder of an unnatural adolescence—caught in the timeless shadows—of words unsayable and acts uncompleted. Through the involuntary mediation of my children, I had completed the usual leap forward, the blind rational leap behind which I now had to limp along. I wasn't ready—neither of us was ready—for old age. This seemed my imagination; my mother wanted always to appear the same, and, just as I had erased myself to support the public figure of my husband, I now had to sustain her in her pride. Throughout the day I'd wonder: "And me?"

Unlike my children I couldn't smile affectionately at her stubbornness, her ostentatious displays of virtue, her small deceptions; I couldn't fail to see intention and purpose in her actions. As if she were playing that last card of hers against me (against me alone)—what were my ailments and my hard work in the face of the death she saw advancing—to silence me, as always.

Soon after she was settled at our house, Gianni unexpectedly had to have a gallstone operation.

He had always enjoyed perfect physical health, even in periods when he was stressed by nervous overexcitement. I had learned to pay attention to his sleepless nights (ordinarily he could sleep even twelve hours straight), to his sudden uncontrollable streams of words, but I had never had to worry about the cigarettes he smoked, the irregularity of his hours, his improvident way of living. I envied him that health, but I also counted on it.

That same autumn I had taken care of my mother's move to our house, made sure she found everything ready, the silver polished on the table, the books in order on the shelves. When, shortly before Christmas, Gianni was about to return, after a month in the hospital, I accepted an invitation to stay for three days in Lazio with my friends Vera and Roberto, among the few old friends with whom I still felt at ease.

I got everything ready with the usual care; my children were used to keeping house without me, once the essentials were in place.

My mother greeted the announcement of my departure in silence. As always I had had to overcome my fear to go and tell her. More than a conversation it had been a monologue on my part, she had been silent, never looking at me directly but staring at the corners of her room.

An hour later I was in the kitchen, filling containers with Gianni's diet foods; she looked in.

"Laura's on the phone. She wants you."

She stood in the doorway, slowly rubbing together her small hands resting against her lap, a gesture she made often as if to warm them, but one that just then seemed to me to express a secret satisfaction. Usually she showed me those hands after preparing one of her excellent minestrones for us, complaining every time that her skin was ruined because she'd had to peel and cut up the vegetables.

I went to the telephone in the living room. My daughter was having a difficult pregnancy; she had lost a child in a miscarriage two years earlier and now, in the third month, she had to stay in bed. I hadn't told my mother this; I hid the family troubles from her as much as possible. I don't really know if it was out of concern or so as not to have to endure her anxieties as well as my own.

"Grandmother told me you're going away?"

So my mother had telephoned her; it occurred to me that in fact I hadn't heard the phone ring.

"Three days," I said, "I'm going with Vera and Roberto. I'm tired, you know I spent practically the whole summer in the city with Grandmother."

My daughter was silent. I said anxiously:

"Everything's ready, as usual."

"Papa comes home from the hospital tomorrow," my daughter said, and that was all. I realized—but still was reluctant to believe it—that my mother had called her to complain about my departure, about my leaving the house on her shoulders. On her, who was served meticulously by everyone.

"I'll see him Saturday," I said, "he's doing really well and is glad for me to have a little vacation. I only have these three days."

"Okay, bye," said my daughter, in the colorless, chilly voice of her doubts, and hung up the phone.

At that moment I was swallowed up by an inner convulsion so violent that it emptied me of any reaction that wasn't the fury I had kept inside for years.

She, my mother, who had lived as freely as a man, for whom other women, as for a man, had raised children and grandchildren, like a man drove me back into my place as a servant. She blackmailed me through my sons, my daughter, soliciting their complicity. And like that, just like that, she wouldn't hesitate to ask for Gianni's, so that I would continue to support the architecture she could blend into without owing me anything. She who, the previous summer, groaning with pain every day while I laced and unlaced her orthopedic girdle, had never let a word of blame escape for the silence of my sister, who had gone on a monthlong cruise. But she hadn't failed to exclaim, using a specific and deliberate plural: "My poor daughters, your mother is becoming a burden to you!"

I went to my son Pietro's room. Walking as if thunderstruck, I could repeat to myself, in a frenzy, only the same phrase: "You won't even make a cup of tea for yourself! You won't even make a cup of tea for yourself!"

"I'm not going," I said to him, "it's impossible."

"Why, Mammi, it will do you good!"

"I can't," I said, "your grandmother will make you pay."

"I'll manage with Grandmother."

"No," I said, "you won't. Only I know how to deal with her."

In the weeks that followed, I did my duties toward her tirelessly, as if contracted in a cramp of revenge: I didn't fail to

offer the proper word—hadn't propriety always been important to her?—a soup, a morning tea for the flu, a pill for a
backache, a walk in the early spring sun. She lived with the
daughter she herself wanted: the mean, useful girl.

In the shower, where no one could hear me, I let out my
anger, insulting her aloud. I said as in a litany: "Feces, snot,
pee, don't forget your duties." When, seeing me busy in the
kitchen, she asked me, good-humored and greedy: "What are
you giving *your* sick person today?" For that "your," which
yet again chained me to my family's illnesses and her old age
as if to a natural moment of my life, I could have killed her.

Yet in those months when she was finding me again as
a daughter, I realized that she was beginning to be afraid of
me, of my labors, of my angry, mute bitterness. Time, which
until now had denied us a story, had reversed the roles: I the
mother and she the child. Not the mother I had become for
my children, however, but the mother she had been, inac-
cessible and perfect in the firmament of childhood. And she
feared in me her own lack of love.

Because, simply, that was the certainty that had struck
me as I was going to Pietro's room: "She had never carried me
inside, I didn't exist in her."

To this certainty, small and profound like my enlighten-
ments, my anger gradually yielded; I couldn't help comparing
the frail old woman that my mother was becoming with the
giant figure against whom I conducted my battle. I saw her
protect herself—she who'd been so bold—with the lies and
the silent pout with which I, as a child, had protected myself

from her. This new, unexpected resemblance surprised me and filled me with a sense of guilt, but didn't transform my resentment into generosity. My anger, although spent, in fact lay in my mind like a gigantic boulder that is the reminder of a cataclysm. I couldn't touch anything, I couldn't bear to rummage among my shards and my trash. I lived day by day and couldn't accept myself; even my adolescent diary, which I was rereading, irritated me.

I had picked it up the night my first grandchild was born and had begun to read it as I waited for the phone call from my son-in-law. Leafing through those pages, in which my writing seemed somewhat awkward and alien, I felt that the expected birth reconnected me in some way to that writing, it was—like the birth of Andrea—again an end and a beginning, even if, I said to myself, of a future sustained on whose periphery I would be only a fragment.

Around the same time, that evening on the Po when we'd ended up talking about Waldensian history, Costanza, a consultant at the Italian state broadcasting network RAI, had proposed that I write something.

"Why don't you do a short script on the subject? I'll present it."

"It's a story of men," my friend Luissa had said. "You always write stories about men."

"Not true," I defended myself, "I also write about women."

"We always expect that you'll tell the whole story, but you pass us by."

"I know them too well," I replied, "they don't interest me."

"Write about yourself, for once," Luissa had said.

"I can't write about myself," I'd said, "I'm not ready yet."

It was September, the canning was done, I carried the jars to the cellar. Then I amused myself by writing a script.

After thirty years the mountain people, the forebears of my grandfather Gioanni Daniele, return to walk on the sun-drenched stony ground and the high plateaus, yellow in autumn, the only sound the very faint rustling of dry grass in the wind and the birdlike whistle of the marmots; they cross the mountains at two thousand meters, under the weight of guns and baggage, with their Occitan calls echoing from valley to valley, psalms sung, vines planted among the rocks.

When I finished the script, I handed it in and started to wait. The thing seemed to be going forward; I had some fears. What did I know about films and screenplays? I would have to learn a new language and I would necessarily be pushed into the background, an old and awkward character.

A director from Rome whom RAI chose to make the film got in touch; he was respectful—"I understand that this story is also your story," he had said, and I was stunned for a moment—but he wasn't very clear about the timing or the responsibilities. I began to sniff papist and Roman traps in which I risked having to do a lot work for the glory of others. His Waldensians, in the end, weren't mine. His discussed doctrine in a loquacious and earnest manner, mine are more concerned with the practical elements of defense and survival. No, I said to myself, better to get in line for a monthly paycheck rather than deal with some anonymous character who knows nothing about me and will pay me in unpredictable banknotes, different every month. The paycheck, too, is always different, though not by much; a small, clean government paycheck that certainly won't be related to the work I've undertaken with the scruples required by the Waldensian God: the State should be served properly; only thus, when the moment arrives, alas sometimes inevitable, can one disobey it.

Meanwhile I began to do more extensive research on the subject.

On a clear autumn day I got in the car with my friend Chicchi to go to Balsiglia, where in 1689 a famous battle was fought between the Waldensians and the troops of the duke allied with Louis XIV. In the small café beside the bridge we were served an excellent tea—the best tea to be found in Italian cafés is in the valleys, perhaps to compensate for all the wine guzzled by the Fathers—by a woman who spoke with the high, clear, rolled-*r* timbre of many Waldensian women. The sound of that *r*, in male voices as well—even my Dutch cousin's voice has it—is for me an immediate signal in which I can't separate the fear of rejection from the hope of welcome.

That autumn day, the few old houses across the bridge under the crest of Balsiglia with its four sharp peaks were in shadow and locked up, the small museum was also closed.

We walked up part of the way to observe from across the stream the wooded slopes where three centuries earlier the battle was fought. The family that owned the café was digging potatoes out of the ground in a field a little ways off; the Germanasca descended gurgling. It was the same Germanasca into which three centuries earlier the Tron-Poulat brothers—those who were harvesting their potatoes were also called Tron or Poulat—had thrown the mill's grindstone before leaving, armed, for Swiss exile. They recovered it later from the waters of the stream, as they prepared for the long winter of 1689 in their bunkers.

I looked at them, the Tron-Poulat family, digging potatoes, and again a sense of inadequacy surprised me, similar to the one that had overwhelmed me when the peasant in Angrogna, leading his animals into the stable, had told me we were cousins. The fall day was so intense around me, in the blue of the sky, in the clear air fragrant with thyme and resin, in the gestures of the people who down below were putting potatoes in sacks, that I seemed an imperfect filter for this reality—which is the same, I said to myself, as that of the era of the events I want to narrate. There was no bond between me and that world, which remained outside me. No, the poor, rocky houses in shadow, the four pointed peaks, the woman with the high, clear voice marked by those *r*'s, were not related to me. Their history didn't precede me, I hadn't come from that.

And yet the Western was still there, entire; as then, my heroes weren't always heroic—had I not planned the film precisely so that the Fathers would get down from their pedestal?—and, as then, my Catholics didn't belong to the hated circle of the persecuting authorities and the mute cops.

In fact, today I pay new attention to their motivations, even if I continue to feel antipathy toward official aspects of the Church—the gold, the purple, the hateful chanting, the bureaucratic obsession with rites, and even that Italian literary and political style, with its excessive and deliberately ambiguous use of adjectives, which to myself I call "Catholic."

When, on the screen, the pope looks out his window, my mother, although she doesn't seem at all connected to her origins, sniffs, her habitual expression of scorn, and observes: "Look at that cuckoo!"

Digging among the documents—I sit for hours in the Biblioteca Reale and delight in reading the anti-Waldensian pamphlets of Prior Marco Aurelio Rorengo; his style is rough but vivid, not at all "Catholic," and I find the Fathers quoted in their everyday language, the moods of the seventeenth century, the details of a quarrelsome but not bloody coexistence in that brief period. I take notes and ponder: it seems to me that I am equidistant between the religious arguments of the prior and those of the Fathers (I am, in truth, indifferent as usual to doctrine), although not, naturally, between those of the persecuted and the persecutors.

One night I ask Gianni: "If you were dying, would you want the last rites?" I realize that he reflects before answering in the negative; that hesitation surprises me and distances him from my idea of him, but, I don't know why, compensates me for an earlier response. Seeing the pope on the screen, I was gripped by one of my thoughts and asked him:

"Do you think he believes in it?" and he immediately, calmly, replied, "Of course not!"

One day my daughter has lunch with us. Her baby, a few months old, sleeps in the next room while we eat. Describing my research at the Biblioteca Reale, I cite the four hundred children who were abducted from their families and given to families of solid Catholic faith during the campaign of 1686.

"Four hundred," I say, "never returned, despite their claims."

My daughter turns pale; her freckles go gray.

"Is that true?" she asks.

"Of course it's true."

"I," Laura says, "would immediately become a Catholic."

Catholic? Why not? Our children aren't baptized; we got married in the town hall in Turin and my young communist colleague and friend, tiny in her large tricolor scarf, read the customary formulas. "Let the children decide," we had said.

Suddenly, however, I don't know how to respond to my daughter. That I, rather, would have fled over paths and cliff faces?

When she's gone, I recall the phrase that Vera's grandmother used when speaking to one of her grandchildren who had become a Catholic in order to get married: "You preferred the light of the candle to the light of the sun." I write it down, I find it beautiful, I will use it.

For that matter, I'm constantly finding beautiful phrases that accord with the facts in the documents I'm consulting.

It's 1688, a Catholic farmer who has bought a farm confiscated by the duke from the Waldensians now exiled in Switzerland—forever, it's thought—is sowing when he hears a voice from the other side of the fence: "Hey you, listen! Odin's telling you to sow carefully for next year!"

Or the French Huguenot caught in an ambush: as he climbs the gallows constructed on market day in the main square of Pinerolo, he speaks, praying aloud: "They have bread up at the Balsiglia, and gunpowder and salt and wine and wool from their flocks and blankets and fabric and pots; and around the bunkers canals to let the water flow out. And the God of armies fights on their side. And they have bread and salt and wine." And the people who listen weep in amazement.

I don't weep and I'm not amazed: I narrate.

My *barbetta* arrogance is a bastard arrogance, a pale reflection of the just arrogance of those who have a history. Of the joyful arrogance that burns in the great bonfires lighted every year on February 17th. It's a bastardized reflection that scarcely illuminates my pages, descended as it is through other pages. I'm a Gypsy who goes around in her caravan, telling stories: here are the victims, here the executioners, here the avengers and the happy ending.

And yet I say to myself, I would never become a Catholic, ever.

One morning I write: " ... in Grandmother's garden in Torre Pellice grew herbs brought by my Huguenot great-grandmother from her garden in Provence." Then with my mother I check the names of the herbs, we can't identify the name of the herb that was used with peas.

Now every so often she'll talk to me about when she was a child. A few sentences, spoken almost with bitterness, reflective. She recalls her father's severity: "My father hit me because I confused *b* with *d*. I was four. My grandmother Jeannette—the Huguenot—in the next room said: *'Ah mon Dieu, mon Dieu, mon Dieu'* while I took it."

The finds of domestic archeology regarding my mother's family are scant. There were repeatedly ruptures so sharp, separations and detachments so sudden (my mother, for example, decided in a few days, for reasons that she never completely explained, to leave a teaching job in Italy—where, she told me, they didn't pay her in summer—to accept a job at the University of Riga, in a country, Latvia, at an immense geographic and historical distance from the little valley she came from), that it's difficult to reconstruct a story in which the relations among the main characters intertwine in a complementary, continuous, and evolving manner. Each has his own particular story and is locked into it like a hostile monad. They interact through a contest of merits (where even grammar and dictionary are weapons of perfection) that is never decided because it lacks the single soothing approval, the impossible approval of the *barbetto* God. For a merely passing grade in Latin Grandfather took his daughter out of middle school, while he let his son, who got even lower grades, go to high school. She never forgave him, but even today she says: "I was his favorite, even though he never let it show."

She doesn't hesitate to say bad things about her brother, of whom she was extremely envious; she alludes to their mother's preference for him: "My mother couldn't stand it that I was more intelligent than my brother." She speaks with the conscious violence that one of the Fathers might have used talking about the water of a *bealera*, an irrigation channel, stolen by the neighbor.

Meanwhile I go on writing about Grandmother, who killed the chicken over the stream in the garden. And I see and smell the water running in the garden, in summer, between the stone facing of the banks—a deep smell, like a cellar, different from the smell of the water that pours over the stones of the Pellice and descends, green and clear, in rapid channels toward the factory. Deep as the fragrance of the leaves on the hillside paths between steep high walls of earth held up by rocks and roots; while the sour scent from the sun on the vine leaves is faint.

I'd need an interval, not to fill with something but a truly hollow, empty break, fresh as the hillside paths, where I could find shelter without asking for anything.

I'm at a standstill and not writing when the RAI contract arrives; confirming my initial distrust, it's very vague about terms, doesn't specify what I'm supposed to do. Furthermore—and this really irritates me—a third of the already small sum promised to me has been added to the director's compensation. I'd rather work for nothing than be underpaid.

I telephone immediately and rescind the contract, and to

the director I write a rude, clear letter: my Waldensians will remain mine.

As always when I say no, I'm almost happy and I move on immediately to other projects. Why not make a documentary with interviews in the valleys that were catholicized three centuries ago, the Cuneo valleys, Val di Susa, the valley of Pragelato?

I search for and can't find a book I thought I had on the Cuneo valleys; I take a map and trace some routes. I go back to the scattered pages where I wrote the sentences about Torre Pellice and write: ". . . I remember very clearly the first time I said to myself, I'm happy! I was seventeen and was running down across the lawn."

At first the girl running struggles to gain an outline. My reluctance to portray her originates in my present aversion toward my past, toward exposing it, defining it: an aversion that has a bizarre counterpoint in the persistence with which I pursue the past of others.

I will write about Concettina, a student of mine twelve years ago. The first time I had her read, I noticed, surprised, the *r* that distinctly indicated an unusually correct French pronunciation. Concettina—tall, blond, the blond of grain, not of flax—read with the slightly hoarse voice of many southern children. She was from Puglia, from Faeto, she said, in the province of Foggia. At home she spoke an Angevin dialect (she still pronounced the *h* in *haut*); the priest had the documents from Faeto in the parish, but wouldn't show them to anyone, and at that Concettina smiled.

I didn't tell Concettina that there were probably other documents, too, perhaps in the archive of the inquisition in Trani. In these documents would be the bloody story of Faeto, Waldensian since the Middle Ages and converted by force during the Counter-Reformation. Listening to Concettina read with her fresh, everyday pronunciation, I imagined that in her town people had continued for years to read the Bible secretly in French—or perhaps to recite, handing down the texts orally—and that was why their language had been preserved for so long. Occitan or Franco-Provençal? On that subject Concettina later wrote her thesis. Tall, blond, and beautiful, she married in the church and the priest officiated, as he had for her mother and her mother's mother.

I say to myself that I'd like to investigate her smile and the silences of her people. Investigate what remains, even if it's only a tacit reserve.

But what about me, what remained in me? In me, a bastard without history, who clings to the history of others, who, in the end, doesn't even have Concettina's undetected roots, her tenacious secret "Angevin"?

In fact the Waldensian God never gives up anyone. He pursues and redeems even bastards. And besides, the Fathers have never given up anything in his name, not a piece of land, a wooded slope, a newborn goat, a water source, a strip of cold sky carved out by the window. Why should they give up Concettina or me?

To him, crouching in my mind, I am bound by a pact that contradicts itself because it's imposed and not ratified: a disagreement. A pact of unfaithfulness. A bare pole, planted deep below the surface of minority resentments. In fact the node of unreasonableness (Catholic, never) that I felt gradually swelling inside me as I wrote about the Fathers is wrapped around a denial that, far from bringing me back to their indomitable past, reconnects me to something of myself, remote not in centuries but in repudiations.

This I should retrace, here would be clues to follow and join together in that other book that Luissa asked of me. I have to write about myself.

Some weeks after I'd decided not to sign the contract with RAI and after putting books and notes back on a shelf—like jars stored in the cellar—I again sat down at the typewriter and started this book.

But though I began with the urgency of an inquiry, with the call of the *barbetto* God, other, completely different motives crowded around, in references and recollections. As I went forward, as I checked, had second thoughts, tried to connect, I not only stumbled in my chronological disorder and my geographical inattention but felt the need to find a distance that wasn't simply the past. I would have liked to be able not to divide the narrating I from the past I, not have the one predetermined by the other, point to the signs contained in the circle that was closing. Only in the present—a great present, without walls—would I be able to give unity to the I, but the present refused.

Before me were my life and my book, and more and more every day it seemed that the former could be transmuted and absorbed into the latter. The pages I wrote took on an irrevocable aspect and oppressed me with an ever-increasing intrusiveness.

Typing I heard my mother cough in the next room and walk along the hall, and my intention to portray her, someone so evasive and diffident, seemed a betrayal on my part. Yet another betrayal. When I went out I hid the pages that were ready, and once when she asked if I was writing something I said no. At times it was as if her presence physically overpowered the possibility of writing.

I was realizing that I didn't want to describe her, find suitable terms, re-create important moments. A real stinginess restrained me. I couldn't allow her adventures in which she wasn't my mother, and I tried to crush her under a nagging comparison that I could barely keep from becoming gossip. Happy episodes didn't occur to me, those comic observations (even of herself) in which her sarcasm softened. I didn't know how to evoke her sonorous voice, in which the *r*'s buzzed in the catarrh. I remembered only her silence or the reverse, cutting opinions and tempestuous scenes.

So I hesitated about whether to record facts, diminish, verify—and so, why not, exorcise—or even give it up: I haven't understood, haven't accepted, and don't know how to represent it. Sink yet again under the ice of the winter sea in Riga.

In the end, in that long period of uncertainty I recognized that the lines I had struggled to produce, erase, rewrite were nothing but a deep inner cry for help and would never be able to get past the cry; of the book that should have contended only with itself, I was making an accomplice.

On the other hand I was also turning it into a monument on which conclusions were carved that would comfort and justify myself. A brilliant—and intrusive—restorer who joined together the Gothic stone hands of the Earl of Arundel and his countess wife on their tomb in Chichester Cathedral may perhaps move a public that consoles itself with the peacefulness of death. But that remains a work of restoration that does not concern either the living or the dead. And really, doesn't seeking peace through a book amount to another misrepresentation? Life alone can give peace and war, and the book has only to tell about that.

And so I wrote and rewrote, seeking the path from me to what I wrote and from there to the reader and then from the reader back to the book, extricating me from the writing and the writing from me.

Meanwhile we had had to move and were living in a small apartment on the second floor of an old building in the city center, with vaulted ceilings, deep, sunken windows, very elegant fittings, in winter not much light and in summer a courtyard that was often foul-smelling. I wrote with the bedside lamp on even during the day. I went around among my plants, transported from high up over a luminous, open square to the long, low balcony overlooking a courtyard, deciding whether to water them. I liked when I watered to let the excess rain down into the courtyard.

The three of us remained, my mother, Gianni, and I.

Of those years I can reconstruct moments and brief periods in my mother's last months that were on the whole serene. She and I were in better health, Gianni was as always careful and patient, the children were available and kind; little by little, as age weakened her, my mother began to trust me. Once she praised one of my books and regretted that it hadn't had its deserved success. A few weeks before her death she asked my sister, who had come to see her: "Where's my daughter?" "But I'm here," said Sisi. "Not you, the other one," she replied.

Ill, in bed, and cared for by me, she said suddenly one evening: "Certainly, the Lord spared you nothing."

It was the only time I heard her name God.

Then she added, hesitating, searching for the words: "First your father, then four children to bring up, and then me." She broke off and after two minutes of silence concluded: "You were"—as if speaking of something in the past that she hadn't realized before—"the Waldensian and Sisi the Jew."

And with those words—with which she intended certainly to "do justice to me" and perhaps thank me—she separated us yet again in her heart.

There isn't much I can add, except this: there was certainly a fracture in her—again a rift, an estrangement—between the moral rule that she felt obliged to transmit and her own nature. Released from that duty (hadn't the same obligation led her, now a European, who had married a Jew, to bring me from Riga to the Waldensian church of Torre Pellice so that I could be baptized?), no longer bound, I was saying, by that promise made by others before her, to whom, not voluntarily, she belonged, my mother happily loved my children.

But between her and me was the rule that, unintentionally, from a distance, and secretly, she had had to hand down to me.

Why she wished to impose and pass it on to me in particular I don't know. I could try saying (entering just for a moment into the matter of those mysteries of love that I discovered to be impenetrable as I was reading the description of my sister in a white wig): because she was unable to love me. Was I not both the proof of her failing the rule and at the same time the cause—blameless but undeniable—of her unhappy marriage? Or rather: it's unlikely you'll love someone who reproduces, well or badly, a model that oppresses you and that you compulsively hand down. The one you raise to be your rival.

In me she rejected both what lay outside the rule or contradicted it, and the feared norm that she saw gradually solidify and take shape in my actions, even though at first sight it was deviant and new.

The women in my life were seldom and reluctantly women for me—my grandmother, empathizing with me for a future, inevitable shared injustice, while she provided the pad for my first period, as much as my mother, who gave birth to me and nursed me—but the men, the Fathers, were father and mother to me, example and touchstone; and so the conclusion is the opposite of what I stated to Luissa that night on the Po: I don't know women, I know only men.

Wasn't it the father my mother as an old woman feared in me, wasn't it the Fathers, in her, I was unfaithful to?

Furious rages against men continue to overwhelm me—uncontrollable rages, when I get up to speak, to cry out, because of an unjust act, a boast, an abuse of power, a mockery of someone who is younger or can't defend herself. I've never loved men older than myself and only the voice of the tenor or even the countertenor seduces me, even though, singing to myself, I sing in a bass voice Verdian arias for great old men. But I shout and weep against the women who weren't women for me, rather than against men.

Through women the Fathers have reached me, walking over the stony ground, and handed over the rocky fragments of their inheritance, the bastard, unfaithful *barbettaggine*, passed down through the centuries by the forebears of my grandfather Gioanni Daniele, a harsh, stingy but inalienable bequest.

Absent from my life in different ways, father and mother, symbolic ghosts, both stamped it indirectly and involuntarily with a black mark, not even imprinting that themselves, my mother with her inability to accept me, my father with his tragic death.

Symbolic ghosts that stealthily haunted my affections, not in order to be revived as real earthly semblances but, on the contrary, in order to endow those affections with their own familiar but elusive qualities; stronger than the presence of the beloved was the grip that wanted to hold love tight. Only as a mother of children (both mine and others') did I escape that deception.

On the other hand, familiarity with the symbol as such, and its innate autonomy, roused in me the need to transform, the impulse to represent, to re-create, the conviction that everything can be reproduced and portrayed.

Not in a tapestry with threads of silk and gold: my unicorn is still always a stray dog sleeping in the July heat in the cool shadow of a closed newsstand.

Two years had passed since my mother's death; I had decided to retire. I was again revising my autobiography during a stay with Andrea in Bordighera. Now with my mother no longer alive, when I reread it, there was indeed a temptation to yield to the past: protagonist, antagonist, story, conclusion. Maybe it would have been easier to entrust the process of that difficult separation to the irrevocable event.

I was having terrible dreams: I was confronted by something that had the aspect of my mother in old age, and I tried to cut it in pieces with a hatchet; while I tried in vain to destroy it, the thing, spurting blood, continued to proclaim that it was my mother, while, crying and screaming, I called out: "Come and tell her that you're the real one, that you're dead, that you're not her."

I could, truthfully, have drawn consolations from our last encounter, attributing it to the will of our common Inscrutable, but I disputed this right with memory and chance, I couldn't make up my mind to give up the present, and the weight of my anger, although spent by now, was still in the present: the hatred that had fought beside us, like Siegfried beside King Günter, hidden in its enchanted cape, that had driven us one against the other in an inherited strug-gle—image against image, not person against person—in a competition of useless merits, on behalf of those who had preceded us.

The last time I spoke to her I had gone to see her in the facility on the hill where she had spent the summer. It was mid-September, and a nurse had called me, worried because she had refused to eat for several days. I went with my son Paolo, who as a doctor had taken care of his grandmother in those years. A few days earlier she had said to me, "I don't feel like reading anymore," and I had had a kind of presentiment.

Paolo examined her and reassured her. Lying dressed on the bed (I noticed that she hadn't taken off her nightgown, which stuck out from the neck of her dress), she listened to him, almost distracted. She said, looking at her arm: "You can see my veins." They brought some broth and I managed to make her eat by spoon-feeding her.

I told her that she had to try to eat at least the broth in the next days, if she wanted to be strong enough to come home on the weekend, where her room with her things was waiting for her. Again she listened distractedly. We said goodbye and moved toward the door. When we were on the threshold, she said, still lying down, barely moving her head toward us, illu-minated by the grand September sky, the red sunset behind the big window spilling light on the bed: "I know you all carry me in your heart."

That July in Bordighera, it never stopped raining. Andrea was at home, studying for an exam, and I was happy to be able to look after him. It was impossible to go to the beach and I walked in rain shoes along the streets incongruously bordered by gardens flowering under a gray November sky.

One afternoon I took a walk to see a large uninhabited villa that interested me and that I returned to look at year after year.

It rose high on the hill, an immense slanted rectangle eroded by time, especially the balconies and under the gable ends of the roof; the shutters on the innumerable windows were dilapidated. The big garden that separated it from the street was now thick with chaotic green vegetation devoid of other color. In the midst of the other gardens—cared for, cultivated, rich in flowers of every species, with lemons, jasmine, infinite geraniums, dahlias, convolvulus—the garden in front of the vast structure was completely consumed by its random disheveled green. An abandoned hotel, I had said to myself; but a name on an oval plaque above the big gate belied this reassuring hypothesis. It was written in ornate—also very tall—pointed bronze letters that said: *"Angst."* This was repeated on the roof in large rusty letters: the *A* was upside down and threatened to drag with it the adjacent consonants.

This time I noticed just before the building an uphill street I'd never seen; in fact when I set off to see it I always expected not to find it anymore—fallen in on itself, collapsing within the still rigid and gigantic geometric structure whose outlines might remain sketched in the air even after its complete disappearance—and I gazed upward until I saw it rise, doors and windows closed and corroded behind the yard without flowers.

So I ascended, under my umbrella, still passing houses with flowering yards. A soft wind had risen from the southeast. Right after the first bend, I found an open gate and saw very close, on the lower side, the immense structure at the end of a grassy driveway. Still I continued for some minutes on my street; there was a long, splendid hedge of purple clematis on the fence of the next garden and a little farther on, behind the villas, a completely wild valley, flowering with broom.

I went back, as I did in those days, to my work of rewriting, to my attempts to close the gap between life and book—it should be a casual, inconclusive conversation among several interlocutors, I said to myself: me, the book, the others, those who appear in it, those who would read it—and there came to mind details, episodes, words I hadn't even cited, maybe as important as those I had. And in the future might there not also be my winter trip to Torre Pellice, which I had found in the afternoon already submitting to the dark protection of Monte Vandalino? The street from the station to the library, where I was going to consult texts, was empty; only a strong wind swept up dry leaves in the gray and violet air. And yet it had seemed to me, cold and alone, that I was reentering a shadowy womb, not welcoming but known, mine.

When I turned back from the flowering valley, I stopped at the gate. I closed the umbrella, since a large ficus extended its thick-leaved branches over my head. I realized that the villa to the left of the gate also, in fact, behind an apparently intact façade, had a caved-in roof. I considered the big building, so close this time, and went over in my mind the innumerability of its rooms—had they been emptied of their past?—under the enormous *A*, upside down like a fallen weapon.

Behind me the ficus leaves blown off by the wind hit the ground with a sharp thud. It was the only sound I heard. "I could go on rewriting forever," I said to myself, as I went on opening the barred doors inside the huge "Angst," "and never be finished." The soft wind mixed smells of wet earth with the smacking thuds of the leaves. "That's not an autumn sound," I thought, "too sharp and distinct," and, turning my back on the lopsided gate, I delivered the pages of a story I would perpetually revise.

MARINA JARRE was born in 1925 in Riga to a Latvian Jewish father and an Italian Protestant mother. She spent her childhood in Latvia until 1935, when her parents separated and she moved to Italy to live with her maternal grandparents. By the time of her death in 2016, Jarre had written over a dozen novels, short story collections and works of nonfiction, of which *Distant Fathers* is hailed as her masterwork.

ANN GOLDSTEIN is a New York-based editor and translator, renowned for her work on Elena Ferrante's Neapolitan Quartet. A former editor at the *New Yorker*, Goldstein has also translated works by Primo Levi, Jhumpa Lahiri and other great Italian language writers.